*"Not even all that has been said prepared me for this place,
its beauty, its splendor, its amazing possessions! I have
walked about it and measured the towers thereof and it is
one long tale of delight."*

Sarah Whitman, 1894

1989 edition, edited by Susan M. Ward and Michael K. Smith,
© The Biltmore Company

Asheville, North Carolina

Introduction

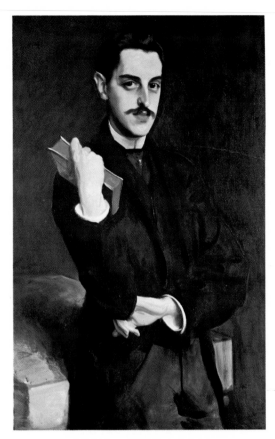

GEORGE W. VANDERBILT, *by J.S. Sargent*

George W. Vanderbilt brought together the genius and talents of Richard Morris Hunt and Frederick Law Olmsted to help him create Biltmore Estate. For both Hunt and Olmsted, Biltmore was the culminating project of their careers. For Vanderbilt, it was a chance to showcase his knowledge and progressive ideals, as well as his collection of art and antiques. Today's guests to Biltmore Estate can take pleasure in the results of these great minds at work. Biltmore Estate represented the pinnacle of thought and ideas at the time of its creation. Today, Biltmore Estate represents the best of preservation through private enterprise. The revenues needed for the preservation of the estate come solely from the estate's commercial operations, making this National Historic Landmark one of the few historic sites in America still privately owned and completely self-supporting. Biltmore Estate receives no form of government subsidy, grants, or trusts. Further, it pays all property taxes and is one of the largest employers in the area.

Today, Biltmore Estate's management endeavors to keep Vanderbilt's vision of a working, self-sufficient estate a viable operation in our modern world. Successful operation in past years has enabled exploration of new business opportunities. We have established vineyards, begun a food and beverage service, expanded our agricultural program, and opened a major winery. The income generated by these modern adaptations makes possible a high caliber approach toward the conservation and maintenance of Biltmore Estate.

An emphasis on historic accuracy is focused on Biltmore House and its 70,000-object collection, as well as the extensive gardens and grounds surrounding the house. The entire Estate is maintained with a respect for the original integrity of the designers and builders. This approach to preservation perpetuates Vanderbilt's philosophy of self-sufficiency and preserves an important American legacy for future generations.

THE VANDERBILT FAMILY

The history of the Vanderbilt family in America begins with Jan Aertson Van Derbilt, a Dutch farmer who came to America in the late 17th century. His descendants were content to follow the pursuit of agriculture, until the day young Cornelius Van Derbilt changed forever the course of his family's history. During Cornelius' lifetime, the family name would be raised from relative obscurity to be associated with great wealth.

Born May 27, 1794 on Staten Island, N.Y., Cornelius, the second son of Cornelius and Phoebe Van Derbilt, asked to borrow $100 from his mother for the purchase of a small sailing vessel, with which he hoped to start a small ferry business. He was operating three ferries at the end of his first year of enterprise. The Vanderbilt fortune had begun.

Recognizing the advantages of steamships over sailing vessels, Cornelius was able to build on his early financial success in such a manner that by 1839, he was able to move his growing family from New York City to a princely residence on Staten Island overlooking the bay. By this time the press had already started calling Cornelius the "Commodore" because of his strong will and determination, qualities which led to his success in commercial endeavors. In 1846, the family moved to a new home at 10 Washington Place in New York City. Cornelius soon turned his attention to rail transportation, and by 1867, he had consolidated his

CORNELIUS VANDERBILT
(1794-1877)

control of the New York Central Railroad, which enabled him to control the major railroad lines between New York and the Great Lakes. Sophia, his wife of 53 years, died in August, 1868, and a year later, Cornelius Vanderbilt married Miss Frank Crawford, eloping to New London, Ontario, for the ceremony.

Cornelius Vanderbilt began a family tradition of financial contributions to worthy causes. His best known contribution was to the Central University of the United Methodist Episcopal Church of the South, in Nashville. Vanderbilt was influenced by his second wife, Frank, to bestow $1,000,000 on the university, which was headed by Frank's cousin, Bishop McTyeire. In gratitude, Bishop McTyeire renamed the school Vanderbilt University.

William Henry Vanderbilt was Cornelius and Sophia's fourth child and first son, named for William Henry Harrison, the Indian fighter who later became President. As a young man, he did not give any indication of the business acumen which was later to gain him respect and wealth. He was quiet, patient, and conservative in his actions, and began working at the age of 18 for the banking firm of Daniel Drew. He did not complain about his salary, though in his first year as a clerk he earned but $100. At 19, he married Maria Louisa Kissam, the daughter of a respected Brooklyn clergyman. He did well in his work at the bank, but became ill. On the recommendation of his physicians, the Commodore was persuaded to purchase a farm for William Henry on

WILLIAM HENRY VANDERBILT
(1821-1896)

Staten Island, exposing him to the therapeutic, country air. Within a few years, he was doing quite well raising crops. One employee said William, "was a downright square man, sociable, reliable, honest, prompt to pay, quick to recognize merit."

Although William was anxious to take a more influential role in his father's affairs, he was reluctant to leave the family farm he had successfully managed for twenty years. His eight children had been born in the farmhouse, which he had enlarged in 1855. He had also achieved recognition in the community as a man of substance and of leadership. In 1864, he did decide to move his family from the Staten Island farm to New York City where he took a more active role in his father's business.

William slowly gained the confidence of the Commodore, who became content to leave details of the daily business to William, but who continued to handle financial and real estate matters. William's attention to detail and his prior financial experience enabled The New York Central Railroad and other Vanderbilt holdings to grow. William Henry, like his father, also contributed money to several causes, including funds for the construction of the College of Physicians and Surgeons, known today as the Medical School of Columbia. He also contributed to Vanderbilt University.

Following the advice and direction laid out by his father who died in 1877, the family business prospered under William's guidance. But his attention was not dedicated solely to business and finance. He also developed an interest in the arts. Beginning with an appreciation for classical music, which led to the founding of the Metropolitan Opera House, William became interested in collecting fine art. A catalog published in 1886 listed 211 paintings in his collection, including works by Millet, Boldini, Corot, Dore, and Turner.

In 1885 William decided that the remains of the Commodore and his descendants should lie together in a mausoleum on a hill overlooking New York Harbor. He purchased a small amount of land on a hill in the Moravian Cemetery at New Dorp on Staten Island, commissioning the architect Richard Morris Hunt to design the tomb. Hunt modeled the tomb after the Chapel of Saint-Gilles at Arles, France.

On Saturday, November 28, 1885, during a meeting with a business associate at his Fifth Avenue home, William Henry Vanderbilt collapsed and died, apparently from heart failure.

William's youngest son, George Washington Vanderbilt, III, was born in the Vanderbilt farmhouse in New Dorp, Staten Island, on November 18, 1862, the youngest of eight children. A shy, quiet person, he exhibited little interest in business affairs. Influenced by the collection of art and antiques in his father's home, he began collecting books and art objects at an early age. After his mother died, George was to inherit the family home at 640 Fifth Avenue and all the art objects within it, including the large collection of paintings his father had assembled.

George had no interest in the social world that had so captivated the Vanderbilt family, preferring instead the adventure of travel and the world of books. On a trip with his mother, he visited Asheville, N.C., a fashionable resort in the 1880's. Here he decided to create a home for himself, a refuge from the tumult of the city.

During the five years of the construction of Biltmore Estate (1890-1895), and during the first few years Vanderbilt occupied the House, he was a bachelor. In 1896, Vanderbilt left for a trip to Europe where he met Edith Stuyvesant Dresser. On June 1, 1898, they were married in a civil ceremony in Paris, where Edith had been liv-

ing, followed the next day by a religious ceremony at the American Church. One hundred-fifty guests attended, including his cousin Consuelo, Duchess of Marlborough. The ceremony was marked by its simplicity, with six bunches of white roses for decoration, and the church organ furnishing the music.

Upon George and Edith Vanderbilt's arrival at Biltmore Estate after the wedding, estate employees met them at the train station and escorted them through an entrance gate made of flowers and on to Biltmore House. Their only child, Cornelia, named for her paternal great-grandfather, was born August 22, 1900.

GEORGE AND CORNELIA
VANDERBILT, September 1900

EDITH AND CORNELIA VANDERBILT, c. 1905

The Vanderbilts were beloved by their employees at Biltmore. An active interest in the estate, the people, and the surrounding area brought about changes and improvements. George Vanderbilt established the first school of scientific forestry management practices in the United States. He also brought modern farming techniques to the relatively rural area surrounding his estate. Edith took a particular interest in assisting the economically disadvantaged families in the region. She taught classes in health care and sewing skills, and visited women who were sick or pregnant, bringing baskets, food, and medicine. The Vanderbilts also started Biltmore Industries in 1901. In this apprenticeship program, young people were instructed in skills to produce small furniture items, baskets, needlework, and woven fabric for resale.

George Vanderbilt maintained an active involvement in the management of the estate until his untimely death in 1914. He was in Washington, D.C. for an appendectomy, and was recovering quite well from the operation. On the afternoon of March 6, he had chatted with Edith and Cornelia during a cheerful lunch. Late in the afternoon, he suddenly fell unconscious, and died within the hour. He was buried in the family vault on Staten Island. In the memorial service for George Vanderbilt held at All Souls Church in Biltmore Village, the following remarks were made:

> "Courteous in manner, dignified in deportment, kind in heart and pure in moral, he was beloved by his friends, honored by his acquaintances and respected by everyone. The place he occupied in the life of this community and in the history of this Church can never be filled. The place will know him no more; but wherever there is nobility of character, wherever there is gentleness of spirit, wherever there are all those things that make for Sweetness and Light, there George Vanderbilt has found his home."

After Mr. Vanderbilt's death, his wife Edith deeded a large portion of the Estate to the United States government. This land became a part of Pisgah National Forest. Other portions of the Estate were also sold, and today the Estate comprises approximately 8,000 acres.

In 1924, Cornelia Vanderbilt, George and Edith's daughter, married The Hon. John Francis Amherst Cecil, third son of Lord William Cecil, the Marquess of Exeter, a direct descendent of William Cecil, Lord Burghley and High Treasurer to Queen Elizabeth the First. Their two sons, George Francis Amherst Vanderbilt and William Amherst Vanderbilt, were born at Biltmore. William, the youngest son, today owns and operates Biltmore Estate, and is a leading advocate of private preservation of historic structures in America.

ESTATE HISTORY

When George Vanderbilt visited Asheville in 1888 with his mother, the mountains of western North Carolina were considered a beautiful respite from urban life. Passenger train service had come to Asheville in 1880, making this southern Appalachian town a day's journey from New York. A mild climate, fresh mountain air, and hot mineral springs nearby made the area a popular resort.

Asheville captivated Vanderbilt. In 1888 he began purchasing land for his estate, eventually totalling 125,000 acres. Vanderbilt created a country estate based on European traditions, especially those in England, where the estate was meant to reflect the significance of land ownership, wealth, the pursuit of physical well-being, and the importance of family and friends. Biltmore Estate would exemplify these ideals.

Vanderbilt's concept for a home, as well as its location, differed from that of his family. His father had built a house on Fifth Avenue in New York, one brother was building a house on the Hudson River, and two of his other brothers were building homes in Newport, Rhode Island.

Vanderbilt's sister, though, was creating a model farm in the Adirondack Mountains in Vermont. Lila Vanderbilt, next in age to George, married Dr. Seward Webb and together they created Shelburne Farms in Vermont. Planning and purchasing of land for Shelburne Farms began in 1886. Shelburne had prize-winning horses and dairy herds. Land conservation practices were also implemented. It seems likely that Vanderbilt was intrigued and influenced by the Webb's undertaking.

LILA AND SEWARD WEBB

Vanderbilt was establishing a strong individual identity by creating a country estate in North Carolina, away from his family in the northeast. Also, he had grown up traveling throughout Europe, where, for centuries, the nobility had been creating grand country estates. Vanderbilt would have participated in elaborate house parties, including many indoor and outdoor activities, at these European estates. He also enjoyed being surrounded by his family and friends and therefore built on a scale that was large enough to entertain everyone. He desired a place to showcase his growing collections of books, art, and decorative art objects in which he had been interested since childhood. These many influences resulted in the concept of a self-sufficient, working estate that was also a country home where he could entertain his guests.

The creation of Biltmore Estate was a monumental undertaking. The talented

RICHARD MORRIS HUNT

BILTMORE HOUSE, November 1892

people that created the Estate focused around Vanderbilt the owner; Richard Morris Hunt (1828-1895), the architect; and Frederick Law Olmsted (1822-1903), the landscape designer. There was cooperation, friendship, and respect between Vanderbilt, Hunt, and Olmsted, with Vanderbilt being the visionary focusing the men on the same goal. The three men combined their accumulated experiences, knowledge, and expertise to produce a uniquely American country estate.

Hunt was one of the foremost architects of the nineteenth century, who received his formal architectural education at the Ecole des Beaux Arts in Paris. He designed private residences and public buildings, and actively promoted architecture as a profession. Buildings designed by Hunt include the base of the Statue of Liberty, the Tribune Building in New York, and the Yorktown Monument in Virginia. He was also the architect for palatial private homes built for wealthy families. Hunt's work for the Vanderbilts included not only Biltmore, but also the Breakers and Marble House in Newport, Rhode Island.

BILTMORE HOUSE CONSTRUCTION CREW, c. 1893

FREDERICK LAW OLMSTED

Olmsted had a similarly impressive background. He was the preeminent landscape designer in America. The Olmsted firm had worked on parks and university campuses throughout the United States, including Boston, Montreal, and Chicago park systems and Stanford, Amherst, and Cornell University grounds. One of his most notable accomplishments had been Central Park in New York City. He also knew the Vanderbilt family from his previous work on the Vanderbilt mausoleum on Staten Island, and from his landscaping of George Vanderbilt's home in Bar Harbor, Maine.

Biltmore Estate derived its name from "Bildt", the region in Holland from which the Vanderbilt family originated, and "more", the Old English word for rolling upland country. Vanderbilt's estate was to incorporate all the entertainment aspects of the country estates in England, adding the concepts of improving the land and the skills of the people in the area. The original 125,000 acres were to include formal gardens, agriculture, and a village, all centered around a 255-room mansion.

OLMSTED, VANDERBILT AND ROAD CONSTRUCTION CREW, c. 1892

When Olmsted began working with Vanderbilt and Hunt at Biltmore Estate, he recommended formally landscaping only the two hundred acres immediately surrounding the house and to turn the remainder into managed forest and farmland. Olmsted recognized the need for repair and control of one of the estate's chief resources—the forest. The land Vanderbilt bought was woodland that had been slashed, burned, and overgrazed. Under Olmsted's direction, Gifford Pinchot was brought in to establish practices of forestry conservation which he had learned in France. Later, Dr. Carl Schenck of Darmstadt, Germany, brought his knowledge of German forestry techniques to Biltmore. The rehabilitation of the forest at Biltmore was without precedent in this country.

The forestry efforts at Biltmore were part of the early land conservation movement in America. In addition to management of the forest, the Biltmore School of Forestry was begun as a place to train foresters in this country. An article in 1914 referred to the Biltmore School of Forestry and Vanderbilt by saying, "There has been a great change in attitude since the Biltmore School was established. It formed an object lesson that forest conservation was not only sane within itself, but also profitable."

The farm operations on Biltmore Estate originally included both horticulture and animal husbandry. The concept of a self-sufficient estate was encouraged through the growing of potatoes and corn and the raising of sheep, pigs, dairy herds, and chickens. Specially-designed outbuildings were built on the estate for the agricultural endeavors.

The immense Estate was also to include a village. This concept was inspired by European estates with their accompanying villages. Biltmore Village, originally the town of Best, was purchased in 1889 by Vanderbilt. At that time, the town consisted of a railway station, two small inns, a grist mill, and a few houses. Construction of the village was underway by 1896. Biltmore Village included cottages,

BILTMORE VILLAGE UNDER CONSTRUCTION, c. 1898

shops, a school, a post office, All Soul's Church, the train station, a laundry, a hospital, and the Biltmore Office Building. The brick sidewalks, attractive street lights, and cohesive architecture created a picturesque village.

The focal point of Biltmore Estate was, and still is, Biltmore House. Hunt designed Biltmore House in the Francis I style, after the 16th-century French chateaux in the Loire Valley. The Chateaux of Blois, Chenonceaux, and Chambord were the prototypes for Biltmore House. Vanderbilt and Hunt created a significant architectural monument and filled it with fine and decorative arts. The two of them supplemented Vanderbilt's previous collection of books and antiques on buying trips to Europe where they purchased objects for Biltmore House. The end result was a 22,000-volume library, furniture from various countries and time periods, an extensive print collection, and sculpture and paintings from important artists.

Throughout construction of Biltmore Estate, there existed a sense of mission, a positive spirit, and a strong sense of comaraderie. The major portion of the construction, undertaken by hundreds of workers, took place between 1890-1895. A brick factory and a woodworking factory were built on the estate. Limestone was brought from Indiana. A three-mile railway spur was built to bring supplies from the main train depot up to the construction site. Exotic, imported materials, walk-in refrigeration, electricity, advanced plumbing, and central heating were all part of the final result of Biltmore.

When the major portion of the construction had been completed, Vanderbilt opened Biltmore House to his friends and family, during Christmas, 1895. A tree stood in the Banquet Hall decorated with presents for the children of employees. A coaching party, distribution of mistletoe and holly, and a dinner were all part of the day's activities. Edith Wharton, a friend of Vanderbilt's and a noted writer and interior design expert wrote to a friend from Biltmore:

> Yesterday, we had a big Christmas fete for the 350 people on the estate—a tree 30 ft. high, Punch and Judy, conjuror, presents and 'refreshments'. It would have interested you, it was done so well and sympathetically, each persons' wants being thought of, from mother to last baby.

ESTATE GUESTS, c. 1900

The Christmas tradition set the precedent for entertainment at Biltmore. In the years following the formal opening of the House, Biltmore became the quintessential setting for recreation and amusement. Indoor activities at Biltmore included

CROQUET IN THE ITALIAN GARDENS, c. 1905

formal dinners and balls on the main floor of the house, while athletic pursuits took place in the basement at the gymnasium, the bowling alley, the swimming pool, and the ping-pong table. Outdoor recreational activities included hunting, fishing, riding, coaching, hiking, croquet, archery, and strolling in the gardens.

Life on a country estate rested on a combination of participation by both guests and servants. The employees during Vanderbilt's time included stablehands, dairy workers, farmhands, and household help. Inside Biltmore House were the steward, the butler, the valet, the cook, the ladysmaid, the housekeeper, the chambermaid, the parlormaid, the laundress, and kitchen staff. About 80 servants worked at Biltmore House and the stable area.

Servants thought of Biltmore as a good place to work. Imagine getting paid better than your peers, working for people thought to be kind and generous, and living at a place like Biltmore! It was the staff that enabled the Vanderbilts and their guests to enjoy all of the activities that were a part of life on Biltmore Estate.

Guests of the Vanderbilts were entranced by their visits to Biltmore Estate. They wrote letters and diary entries praising their visits. Paul Leicester Ford, a nineteenth century author and a friend of Vanderbilt's, dedicated one of his books to George by writing:

> ...and so as I read the proofs of this book I have found that more than once that the pages have faded out of sight and in their stead I have seen Mt. Pisgah and the French Broad River, or the ramp and the terrace of Biltmore House, just as I saw them when writing the words which serve to recall them to me. With the visions, too, has come a recurrence of our games of chess, our cups of tea, our walks, our rides, and our drives. It is therefore a pleasure to me that the book so naturally gravitates to you, and that I make it a remembrance of these past weeks of companionship...

George Vanderbilt's vision became reality. His ideas and planning resulted in construction of a nineteenth-century country gentleman's estate, which became a setting for innovative land usage, as well as an environment for guests to be entertained. Today, the history and the legends of Biltmore Estate continue.

LODGE GATE IN BILTMORE VILLAGE

The entrance to Biltmore Estate is through the LODGE GATE in Biltmore Village. Both its bricks and roof tiles were made on the Estate. Mr. Vanderbilt constructed the Village near the railroad to provide housing and services for his many workers. In addition to All Souls Church, Biltmore Village originally included a hospital, a school, a post office and various shops.

The APPROACH ROAD winds for three miles through a deliberately controlled landscape. The road runs along the ravines instead of the ridges, creating a deep natural forest with pools, springs and streams. Around the last turn, the visitor passes through the iron gates and pillars that are topped by early 19th-century French stone sphinxes, and then into the expansive court of the House.

This room-by-room description is followed by an appendix beginning on page 81 that lists all of the objects in each room, including date and country of origin.

THE WINTER GARDEN, c. 1898

MAIN FLOOR

The marble paved ENTRANCE HALL has walls and arches of Indiana limestone. On the center table, there is an important set of bronzes by the Parisian, Antoine-Louis Barye (1796-1875) who is most famous for his animal sculpture. Mr. Vanderbilt admired the artist's work, of which the house contains many examples. This tablepiece is an interpretation of the poem *Orlando Furioso* written by Ariosto and was commissioned by the Duc de Montepensier, youngest son of King Louis Phillipe. The center sculpture portrays Roger carrying off Angelique on the Hippogriff. The flanking candelabra are supported by the figures of Juno, Minerva and Venus and are crowned by the three Graces.

The WINTER GARDEN is furnished exactly as it was during the Vanderbilts' time at Biltmore House. The bamboo furniture was bought by Mr. Vanderbilt in France from Perret & Fils et Vibert in Paris. In the center is a fountain with a statue of a boy and geese, the work of Karl Bitter, a Viennese sculptor. Bitter came to this country as a young unknown in 1889. His work quickly made a name for him, especially among architects. Some of his other works are the bronze Astor Memorial Gates at Trinity Church and the figures of Architecture, Sculpture, Painting and Music on the front of the Metropolitan Museum of Art, both in New York City.

On the walls just outside the court are copies of the Parthenon frieze which were executed for Mr. Vanderbilt by Eugene Arrondelle of the Louvre, Paris. The ceiling tiles were made by Raphael Guastavino.

THE BILLIARD ROOM, c. 1898

The BILLIARD ROOM is part of a suite of rooms which provided entertainment and a retreat for the men of the household. Through the doors concealed in the paneling of the fireplace wall, there is also a smoking room and gun room. The oak paneling of the Billiard Room is almost covered with sporting and theater prints after the paintings of Landseer, Reynolds, Atkinson, Stubbs and others. Hanging on the left is *Rosita* by the Spanish painter, Ignacio Zuloaga Y Zabaleta.

The oak pool and billiard tables are 19th-century American and were probably made for the room. The leather settees and chairs were made by Morant & Co., London, in 1895. They are copies of the famous 17th-century furniture at the English estate, Knole.

THE BILLIARD ROOM
See Appendix, page 81.

In the BANQUET HALL, the ceiling arches 70 feet above the 72 x 42 foot expanse. The room was designed to display the five unique tapestries which hang on the walls. They tell the lively story of the perilous love affair between Venus and Mars, which was threatened by her husband Vulcan, and humorously treated by the other gods who interceded to restore peace. These are the only known 16th-century Flemish tapestries woven from the Venus and Vulcan designs. The set probably once consisted of at least seven pieces. These were the prototypes for all the famous Venus and Vulcan tapestries, which were woven later in England in the 17th century at Mortlake and Lambeth. No one has been able to assign the designs of the weaving to any one master. Detailed descriptions of each tapestry can be found in the Appendix, page 81.

The tapestries throughout Biltmore House are presently undergoing conservation work. The project is being completed in-house using equipment designed and built by Biltmore employees. The tapestries are being washed, repair stitched and re-lined.

The acoustics of the Hall are so perfect that two people sitting at opposite ends of the Banquet Hall table do not have to raise their voices in order to be heard. Due to the enormous dimensions of the room, both the Banquet Hall table and two throne chairs were especially designed by the architect, Richard M. Hunt. The carved backs of the thrones and *The Return from the Chase* over the huge triple fireplaces are the work of Karl Bitter. High above the fireplaces is the Vanderbilt crest crowned by flags of the great powers at the time Columbus discovered America.

On the opposite wall of the Hall are more carvings by Bitter. A scene from Wagner's opera, *Tannhäuser* adorns the Organ Gallery. The brass and copper pieces below are 18th and 19th-century Dutch, Spanish and French.

The statues of Joan of Arc and St. Louis over the entrance to the Hall are also by Bitter. The Latin motto between them reads, "Give us peace in our time, Lord."

Completing the medieval spirit of the room are trophies of armor over each door and flags hanging gaily above. These flags are replicas of the thirteen original colonies, flags of the Revolutionary War, and the Biltmore Estate World War I Service Flag.

THE BANQUET HALL
See Appendix, page 81.

The BREAKFAST ROOM was used for more informal dining than the Banquet Hall. The walls are Spanish leather. The mantel is of jasperware, and the history of this ware is of interest. In 1767, Mr. Josiah Wedgewood commissioned Thomas Griffiths, a South Carolina planter and student of geology and botany, to look into reports of a quality "Cherokee clay." This was found just north of Franklin, North Carolina, about 60 miles from Asheville, and five tons of it were sent to England. Experiments with the clay produced the now familiar jasperware in blue, green and white.

On the walls are various portraits of the Vanderbilt family. Above the display case is William H. Vanderbilt, father of George W., and hanging above the door on the right is Commodore Vanderbilt, his grandfather. On the table and in the display case are samples of the Vanderbilt's china and glassware. The family dinner service has a gold monogram and was made by the Minton and Spode factories in England. The purple shell form china is Wedgwood Moonlight Lustreware. The dessert sets with hand painted birds are also by Minton and Spode. The crystalware is Baccarat.

On the far left as you enter the MORNING SALON is a chess table and a set of ivory chessmen. The table was owned and used by Napoleon Bonaparte while a prisoner at St. Helena. Very probably, it is the same table referred to in the diary of Dr. O'Meara, a physician who attended the Emperor. According to his memoirs, the table was a gift from Lady Holland. After Napoleon's death, his heart was placed in a silver urn upon the table prior to being placed in his coffin.

The room is furnished with a beautiful set of Louis XV style chairs and sofa covered in petit point as is the French screen on the left. On both walls hang Cardinal Richelieu's hangings mounted on red velvet with his motto *Semper Idem*, armorial bearings and cardinal's hat.

THE BREAKFAST ROOM
See Appendix, page 83.

The MUSIC ROOM was completed and opened to the public in 1976. Up to this time, the room existed with only bare brick walls. The French Renaissance style was chosen for the restoration so that the room would reflect the exterior character of the Chateau, and the designs were skillfully executed by Biltmore Estate craftsmen.

This new room was also designed to display some outstanding art objects. Above the fireplace hangs one of Albrecht Dürer's largest commissions for the Emperor Maximilian I. This *Triumphal Arch of Maximilian* depicts his family tree, scenes from his life and historic portraits of the nobility of the Holy Roman Empire. The work consists of 92 engraved blocks which form a print 11¼ feet high and almost 10 feet wide. Inscribed on the mantel below are the monogram and dates of Albrecht Dürer (1471-1528). The mantel, designed by Richard Morris Hunt, was stored in the house for eighty years before installation.

To the right of the mantel is a rare set of Meissen Apostles. These twelve porcelain figures and candlesticks were modeled by the famous sculptor of the Meissen (Dresden) porcelain works, Johann Joachim Kändler. The apostles, with flying drapery outlined in gilt, are in the baroque manner and are modeled after those in the Lateran Church of St. John in Rome. Complete altar sets were made between 1735 and 1741 for the Empress Amalia and the Empress Maria Theresa of Austria, the Empress Catherine of Russia and Pope Clement XII. The set at Biltmore House is the only complete set still in existence marked with the Austrian crest.

THE MUSIC ROOM
See Appendix, page 84.

Through the Entrance Hall, on the right, is the 90 feet long GALLERY. The room features three tapestries representing *The Triumph of Virtue Over Vice.* The decoration on the fireplaces, the stenciled ceiling and the linen-fold paneling were all stylistic of the 16th century and provide a harmonious setting for the hangings.

MRS. GEORGE VANDERBILT
By Boldini

The Brussels tapestries are of special interest not only for their rare beauty but because, both in design and subject matter, they show the transition from the Gothic influence to that of the Renaissance which typifies the hangings in the Banquet Hall. These three were woven in the first quarter of the 16th century. The feeling is Gothic as is the even distribution of pictorial areas over the entire work,the skyline near the top and the fine pattern of figures in action. However, the growing interest in form, perspective and symmetrical balance belongs to the Renaissance. They are full of Gothic symbolism, but the figures, which are taken from mythology, from Greek, Roman and Medieval history, from the Bible and the Apocrypha are typical of the Renaissance. Detailed descriptions of each tapestry can be found in the Appendix, page 85.

The portrait over the door into the Library is George W. Vanderbilt, painted by John Singer Sargent, who was his personal friend. On the left is a Sargent painting of Mr. Vanderbilt's mother, Mrs. William H. Vanderbilt; on the right is Mrs. George Vanderbilt, by Giovanni Boldini.

THE GALLERY
See Appendix, page 84.

THE LIBRARY, c. 1898

Mr. Vanderbilt was a scholar in many fields and had reading knowledge of eight languages. The LIBRARY contains over 10,000 volumes, while the entire book collection numbers over 23,000. The books, found throughout the house, reflect Mr. Vanderbilt's broad interests. The shelves contain classic literature as well as works on art, history, architecture, and landscape gardening.

The classical-baroque detailing of the room is enhanced by the rich walnut paneling and the carving of Karl Bitter. Over the black marble fireplace, he carved two figures representing Hestia, goddess of the hearth on the left and Demeter, goddess of the earth on the right. Between the figures is a 17-century French tapestry. The Vulcan and Venus andirons in the fireplace were also sculptured by Bitter.

The magnificent ceiling painting, *The Chariot of Aurora,* was brought to America by Mr. Vanderbilt from the Pisani Palace in Venice. The canvas is by Giovanni Antonio Pellegrini (1675-1741) and is the most important work by the artist still in existence. While Pellegrini executed many important commissions, most of his paintings were destroyed in the last war in Europe. By bringing this ceiling to America, Mr. Vanderbilt preserved for the world a key work in the development of 18th-century Italian painting.

THE SECOND FLOOR LIVING HALL

SECOND FLOOR

On the second floor, there are seven guest suites and two master bedrooms, as well as five bedrooms in the *Bachelor's Wing*. The third floor has a similar arrangement. There is a total of thirty-two guest bedrooms in Biltmore House, not including servants' quarters.

At the top of the stairs to the right, is the LOUIS XVI BEDROOM. Both the furnishings and architectural finish reflect the French tastes for opulence just before the Revolution. The period decor has light classical ornament as opposed to the rococo curves of the Louis XV style in Mrs. Vanderbilt's bedroom, seen later on the tour. Both the furniture and walls are in red damask and the Aubusson rugs complete the effect.

The SECOND FLOOR LIVING HALL serves as an upstairs sitting room. On the left wall is a group portrait of the William H. Vanderbilt family by Seymour Guy. The full length portrait on the right is Frederick L. Olmsted, landscape architect of the Estate. Further down the hallway is Richard M. Hunt, the architect of Biltmore House. Vanderbilt brought the artist, John S. Sargent, to Biltmore in 1895 to paint the portraits of the two men who created his Estate. In the middle of these hangs *The Waltz* by Anders Zorn (1860-1920), Swedish painter, etcher and sculptor. Across the room to the left of the fireplace is a painting of a Vanderbilt family yacht by an unknown artist.

THE LOUIS XVI BEDROOM
See Appendix, page 86.

MR. VANDERBILT'S DRESSING TABLE

The handsome SOUTH BEDROOM was Mr. Vanderbilt's. The fireplace is the primary decorative feature of the room, and the tapering pedestals topped with the head and torso of a figure are typical baroque-style elements.

On the upper walls are plaster friezes, urns and busts by Eugene Arrondelle of the Louvre. The brackets, hinges and other hardware were made by a craftsman specially engaged by Mr. Vanderbilt. The dressing table, center table, chairs and sofas were designed by the architect, Richard Morris Hunt, and produced by Baumgarten & Co., New York. The many prints on the walls reflect Mr. Vanderbilt's passion for collecting fine engravings. From the windows of his bedroom, the owner had a magnificent view of his Estate, Mt. Pisgah and all that lay between.

THE SOUTH BEDROOM
See Appendix, page 87.

DETAIL OF 17th CENTURY EBONY CABINET

The OAK SITTING ROOM reflects 17th-century Jacobean splendor with its paneled walls and plaster ceiling of intricate strapwork patterns. The portraits on the wall are by John S. Sargent. On the right in the black dress is Mrs. Walter R. Bacon, a cousin and close friend of Mr. Vanderbilt. The other portrait is his aunt, Mrs. Benjamin P. Kissam.

The large ebony cabinet in the corner was a special product of Antwerp and South Germany in the mid-17th century. Pieces of this type were prized possessions of rich European collectors, and both Anne of Austria and Cardinal Mazarin commissioned similar cabinets. On the shining dark wood, a series of mythological scenes are carved. The two center doors reveal a rich architectural *trompe-l'oeil* interior.

The bronzes throughout the room are by the French sculptors, Barye, Meunier, and Mêne. This group of 19th-century artists are referred to as the "animaliers" because of their subject matter.

THE OAK SITTING ROOM
See Appendix, page 87.

CHINESE GODDESS OF MERCY
IN THE LIVING HALL

As Mr. Vanderbilt was a bachelor when he planned Biltmore House, the NORTH BEDROOM was originally his mother's, Mrs. William H. Vanderbilt. After his mother's death and his subsequent marriage to Edith Styvessant Dresser, the room became his wife's.

The room was decorated in the Louis XV style which was considered appropriately feminine. The furniture and the paneling are full of graceful curves, typical of the rococo period. The walls are of yellow silk; the upholstery is purple and gold velvet.

The engravings on the walls are by French artists of the 18th century such as Willie, Bervic, Drevet and Roger. The rugs are Savonnerie, and their soft colors complete the feminine mood of the room, as does the oval shape.

THE NORTH BEDROOM
See Appendix, page 88.

Mrs. Vanderbilt's BATH AND DRESSING AREA are adjacent to her bedroom. The lilac and pale yellow trim are the original colors of the walls, probably selected to complement the rich gold and purple brocade of her bedroom. The elaborate shower, a rarity in 1895, has complex adjustments to regulate temperature settings. Displayed in the large shelved storage area are delicate French and American linens, most embroidered with the Vanderbilt monogram.

Nearby is the LADYSMAID'S ROOM. Women of Mrs. Vanderbilt's social standing necessitated the employment of a personal ladysmaid. This position required tending to Mrs. Vanderbilt's closets and clothing, assisting her in dressing, running general errands and accompanying her in her travels at home and abroad. From 1912 until 1915, Martha Laube served as Mrs. Vanderbilt's ladysmaid. Accounts state that Mr. Vanderbilt conversed with Miss Laube "mostly in German, of which she had an excellent command."

The wooden box mounted on the wall next to the fireplace is part of an elaborate electrical call system which enabled the Vanderbilts and their guests to call servants from throughout Biltmore House. The origin of the call was indicated by flags in the wooden boxes in servants' areas. The counterpane bedspread in the ladysmaid's room is typical 19th century American, fashioned after the early 18th century quiltwork produced in Marseilles, France. Spreads of this sort were advertised heavily by such mail order houses as Lord and Taylor's by the late 1800's.

With an average of 80 servants at Biltmore Estate, the SEWING ROOM was a busy workplace for all female servants in the house. A house seamstress would organize projects such as sewing upholstery, bedding and draperies. The room was also used for routine mending, darning and handiwork as well as for making some of the servants' uniforms. Floors were left bare in order to more readily retrieve dropped thread, needles and pins. Some examples of original servants' clothing hang in the wardrobe.

THE SEWING ROOM
See Appendix, page 88.

THE MAIDS' SITTING ROOM

The MAIDS' SITTING ROOM is actually located between the second and third floors and was used as a gathering place for both the Vanderbilts' maids as well as those maids traveling with the Vanderbilts' guests. In this room, the women could meet for conversation, reading and light sewing. The room was also, however, a working area, if for nothing more than practicing the art of home remedies and herbal medicine. A ladysmaid was often the 19th century household's resident apothecary, supplying cures for both the lady of the house as well as other female servants under her. The armchairs covered with floral upholstery in this room are of rosewood and date to about 1860.

The beautiful third floor HALLWAY, with its ogee arches, and LIVING HALL are lined with 19th century portrait etchings as well as architectural prints. Hanging next to the living hall fireplace are three works by American artist James Whistler. The first is an oil portrait of Edith Vanderbilt; to the right of the painting are two prints, also by Whistler. Used as an informal setting for the Vanderbilts' guests to have tea, play parlor games, and be entertained by a guest's musical ability on the piano, the Living Hall features three particularly interesting glass-fronted cabinets. All three are from the Fifth Avenue residence of George Vanderbilt's father, William H. Vanderbilt. Also in this room are many items George Vanderbilt collected during his world travels, including elaborately inlaid Japanese swords from his 1892 trip to the Orient. Mr. Vanderbilt was also an inexhaustible collector of fine Eastern carpets. He often bought carpets in volume: one document in the Biltmore House archives indicates he purchased 300 carpets from a London rug dealer at one time.

THE THIRD FLOOR LIVING HALL
See Appendix, page 89.

THE SHERATON ROOM

Each of the next three guestrooms reflects a different style of English furnishings. In the SHERATON ROOM, the painted Satinwood bed is the focal point, and is identical to a plate in Sheraton's design book. Thomas Sheraton, like Chippendale, published several furniture pattern books in the latter part of the 18th century, and the Sheraton style was based on them. Copies of the works of both these designers are in the Biltmore Library.

Other furniture in the room displays the various features of the Sheraton style. The use of inlaid or painted motifs such as a wreath, swag and bow are commonly seen. Tapered legs and crisp outlines are used, as opposed to the curves of the Chippendale style.

The Sheraton Room contains family portraits. Over the fireplace is a portrait of George, Frederick and Eliza Vanderbilt as children, painted in 1867 by Jacob H. Lazarus (1822-1891). On the right wall is the Currier and Ives print of William H. Vanderbilt, George's father, racing his famous trotters, Maud S. and Aldine.

A bathroom separates each of the next two rooms. Even to contemporary eyes, the fixtures seem very modern. In the 1890's, a bathroom in the home was a luxury that few people could afford. A bathroom for every bedroom was astounding.

See Appendix, page 90.

THE CHIPPENDALE ROOM

In the CHIPPENDALE ROOM, the dark mahogany furniture is in the Chippendale style. Thomas Chippendale was the best-known British designer and cabinetmaker of the 18th century. His pattern books were the design inspiration for furniture makers in America, England and other parts of Europe. Details such as the ball and claw foot and rococo curves are most often associated with his furniture designs, although many other decorative elements were also used.

The damask pattern wallpaper was reproduced from an original paper in Biltmore's collection. The coordination of drapery, upholstery and wallcovering was popular in the 18th century.

Over the mantel and on the left wall are two paintings by the French painter, Pierre Auguste Renoir (1841-1919). They are entitled *Child with an Orange* and *The Young Algerian Girl.* The two seascapes are by Maxime Maufra (1861-1918), a French painter of the same period.

See Appendix, page 90.   41

1895 BATHROOM

The OLD ENGLISH ROOM is in a 17th-century style of decoration. The walls are papered in a pattern similar to a Gothic stencil design. The sofa and chairs are reproductions of the 17th-century furniture at Knole House in England. These are complemented with Jacobean style chests and tables.

The room serves as an appropriate setting for the Cecil family portraits. Over the mantel is The Great Lord Burghley, William Cecil (1520-1598), painted in 1589 by Marc Gheeraerts. Lord Burghley was Queen Elizabeth's Lord High Treasurer and was among those responsible for the great Elizabethan era in England. The present owner of Biltmore is a direct descendant of Lord Burghley and continues the Cecil name.

Straight ahead is a portrait of the Cecil children, William and Frances, painted in 1599 by Federigo Zucchero (1543-1609). Between these two 16th-century paintings is their descendant, John Francis Amherst Cecil (1900-1954) by Walter I. Cox. George Vanderbilt's daughter, Cornelia, married John Cecil in 1924.

THE OLD ENGLISH ROOM
See Appendix, page 91.

THE HALLOWEEN ROOM

DOWNSTAIRS (Basement)

The downstairs tour begins by descending from the Staircase Hall to the recreational and working areas of Biltmore House. The first room on the tour is the HALLOWEEN ROOM. It was painted in 1926 by houseguests in preparation for a dance. The decoration took three weeks to paint and each guest took a section to design personally. Presently, the room is an interpretive space focusing on the history, collections, and preservation of Biltmore Estate.

Following is the BOWLING ALLEY. The bowling balls were made of wood and varied in size according to the different games played. The alley is laid with a hard maple floor on the first third where the balls hit and with pine further down where the balls roll. This same formula is used on modern alleys today. These lanes were installed by Brunswick-Balke-Collendere Company in 1895 and according to the company, are probably the oldest still in existence.

THE BOWLING ALLEY
See Appendix, page 91.

THE GYMNASIUM

The 17 DRESSING ROOMS have a separate hallway for ladies and gentlemen. Six dressing rooms are on display here. Each activity of the day had its own dress code, whether it was swimming, taking tea, riding, or dinner, and it was not unusual for a 19th-century lady to change clothes five or more times a day.

All types of recreational activities were planned for Biltmore's house guests as was the custom at the great country houses of the time. Outdoor exercise included riding, coaching, hunting, croquet, fishing, and tennis, as well as walking along many garden paths. In case of bad weather, a recreational space was also included inside the house. The indoor SWIMMING POOL was enjoyed by the ladies and the GYMNASIUM, primarily for the male guests, contains exercise machines, parallel bars and other small equipment.

THE SWIMMING POOL AND A DRESSING ROOM
See Appendix, page 92.

At this point the downstairs recreational area ends and the service area begins. Down the hallway and around the corner from the Gymnasium is the VEGETABLE PANTRY which contains bins of onions, potatoes and other vegetables and fruits. Next is the HOUSEKEEPER'S PANTRY. This is the largest pantry and doubled for the housekeeper's office where it was her job to inventory and order the supplies for the house. Just beyond is the CANNING PANTRY for home prepared fruits and vegetables from the Estate.

Conveniently located down the hall are the SERVANTS' BEDROOMS. The rest of the servants' rooms are on the fourth floor, with the exception of the higher ranking servants. They had their own suites of rooms close to the areas of the house in which they carried out their main duties. Separate halls of bedrooms were provided for each sex and rank of servant. Some of the original livery of the butlers, housemaids and coachmen are displayed in these downstairs bedrooms. The social hierarchy "below stairs" was more strictly enforced than "above stairs." Senior or upper staff members dined and socialized separately and in many cases were waited on by the lower house servants. Traditionally, the chef, butler, housekeeper, personal valet and ladysmaid were among the more privileged class of servants, while the scullery maid, maid of all-work, footman and page were on the other end of the scale.

A SERVANT'S BEDROOM
See Appendix, page 92.

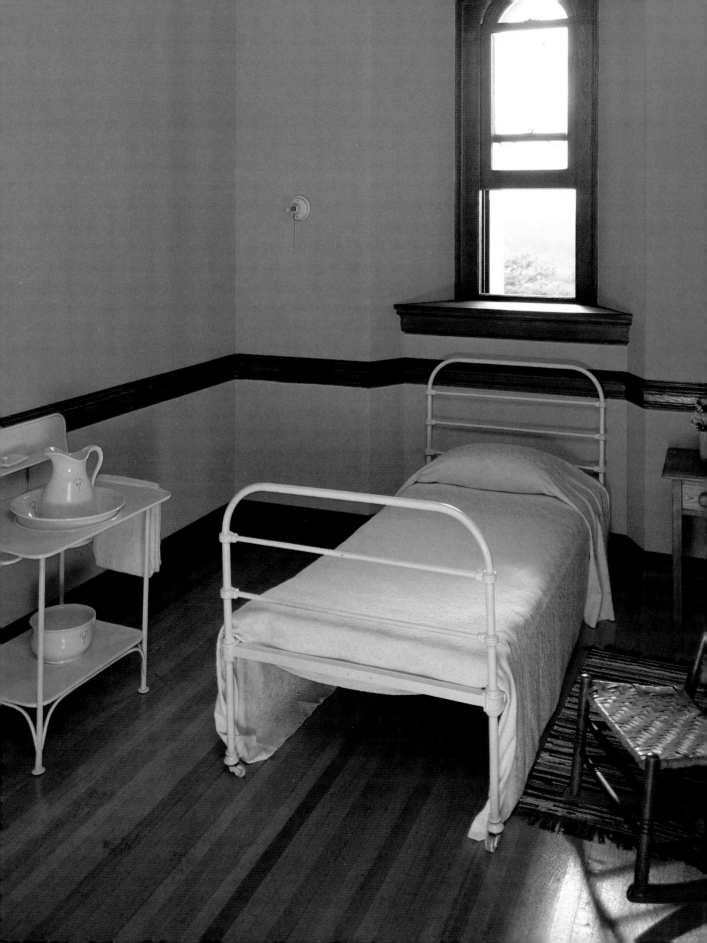

THE ROTISSERIE KITCHEN

The meals were prepared in the next three kitchens and were staffed by an army of chefs, cooks and scullery maids.

Down the hall to the left is the PASTRY KITCHEN where the fine baking was done. A special oven was installed as well as a marble slab table for rolling out dough. The refrigerator was set at a temperature suitable for pastries.

The ROTISSERIE KITCHEN contains an electric rotary spit on which the game course of an elaborate banquet was roasted. Since rotisserie cooking over an open fire was smoky and greasy, it was separated from the Main Kitchen.

THE PASTRY KITCHEN
See Appendix, page 92.

Most of the cooking was done in the MAIN KITCHEN. The large cook stove was heated by coal or wood, and it was the scullery maid's job to start the fires early in the morning before anyone else was awake. The original copper pots and pans hang on a rack over the main work table. The kitchen staff would lay out the work table with utensils in readiness for the chef. Other interesting kitchen antiques such as a coffee mill, a sausage stuffer, a giant mortar and pestle and period food tins are on display.

THE MAIN KITCHEN
See Appendix, page 93.

SMALL PANTRY

The KITCHEN PANTRY has an electric dumbwaiter on the right that transported food up as high as the fourth floor. The hand-operated dumbwaiter on the left carried food up to the Butler's Pantry, adjacent to the Banquet Hall on the first floor.

The SERVANTS' DINING ROOM is one of a number of dining areas for the staff. Together, the house and stables had a staff of 80 servants. The SERVANTS' HALL is the downstairs version of the Guests' Living Hall. The servants gathered here while waiting for their call to duty.

The early WALK-IN REFRIGERATORS were cooled by an ammonia gas and brine water solution which was pumped through pipes inside the refrigerators. The machinery for the refrigeration system and an ice plant were located in the sub-basement. Down the hall is the TRUNK ROOM.

THE MAIN LAUNDRY

Next is the WORK ROOM where the flowers for the house are arranged by the staff floral designer. Flowers and plants from the gardens and greenhouses have always been an important part of Biltmore's decoration.

The following rooms on the right are the BROWN LAUNDRY which was used for hand laundry or for the staff's laundry, and the LAUNDRESSES TOILET.

The MAIN LAUNDRY has equipment similar to the original machinery that was installed in 1895 and was very modern for its day. The barrel washer, extractor, ironing mangle, and wash tubs came from Troy Laundry Machinery Company when the house was built. Vast amounts of table and bed linens were generated by Biltmore's large staff and many house guests; therefore, its design was similar to that of a commercial or hotel laundry of the period.

A separate IRONING ROOM is on the far side of the Main Laundry, and on the right is a DRYING ROOM with pull-out racks and electric coils for drying the clothes. This was also installed by Troy Laundry Machinery Company.

THE DRYING ROOM

THE TROPHY ROOM

FIRST FLOOR

At the top of the Bachelor's stairwell is the SMOKING ROOM. The book-lined walls and fireplace provide a comfortable retreat for the gentleman's after dinner cigar and brandy. Since ladies did not smoke, this section of the house was an all male retreat. The sleeping quarters for the single male guests are on the upper floors of this section.

The TROPHY ROOM contains glossy ebonized paneling and cabinets with gun racks and bird trophies. Shooting was a popular country house activity. Mr. Vanderbilt had the estate stocked with deer, birds, and other wild game to provide his guests with an interesting day's hunting.

The walls of the Entrance Hall to the Bachelor's Wing are lined with architectural prints by A. H. Haig (1835-1921). This doorway, used in bad weather instead of the main entrance, was through the *Porte Cochere,* a covered carriage entrance.

After exiting the main portion of Biltmore House, continue your visit by walking left into the courtyard and STABLE.

THE SMOKING ROOM
See Appendix, page 94.

THE STABLE

Opened in July 1987, the STABLE complex at Biltmore reflects the significance of horses and carriages as both means of transportation and recreation. George Vanderbilt's stable was surely one of the most modern with such features as electricity, indoor plumbing, glazed brick walls, and concrete flooring, as well as the standard brass fixtures and hardware.

In the REPAIR ROOM, you will find several original pieces of stable furniture, including a harness cleaning and repair rack, which was used to hold and store harness while it was being cleaned, stitched, and treated by a full-time repairman.

In the BLANKET ROOM are many original horse blankets and carriage lap blankets, many of which are hanging on wooden and brass fixtures made for airing and drying out the blankets.

The SADDLE ROOM, with its many mahogany and brass saddle and bridle brackets, housed all of the Vanderbilt saddles, including three sidesaddles used by Edith Vanderbilt. The girth stretcher, saddle horse, and saddle airer were made in 1987 by the Biltmore Furniture Conservation Shop as reproductions of late nineteenth century stable necessities.

The HARNESS ROOM, the largest of the four museum display rooms, was used for storing and cleaning carriage harness. On the far wall is a glass and wood display case where polished steel bits and chains would have been displayed.

In addition to the four display rooms are two others: the CARRIAGE HOUSE and the STABLE. One of the twenty carriages kept at Biltmore was an *omnibus*, especially made for Mr. Vanderbilt in France, which could carry up to fourteen passengers. The Stable, opposite the Carriage House, contained approximately thirty of Mr. Vanderbilt's prized driving horses, which were kept in either box or standing stalls. Today the retail sales area is located in the Carriage House, while the Stable Cafe, which offers light refreshments, is located in the Stable.

THE SADDLE ROOM
See Appendix, page 95.

THE GARDENS of Biltmore Estate are as diverse as the plants they contain. Designed by the great American landscape architect Frederick Law Olmsted and supervised for 60 years by Chauncey Delos Beadle, they run the gamut from the formal manicured look of the English Walled Garden to the natural informality of The Ramble.

Adjacent to Biltmore House are the LIBRARY TERRACE and ITALIAN GARDEN. The Library Terrace, which is covered with old wisteria and trumpet creeper vines, once looked over a lush bowling green. Today it looks out over a swimming pool surrounded by a fine boxwood hedge. On the horizon rises Mount Pisgah, once part of the Estate and now a part of Pisgah National Forest. Decorating the terrace are statuary, a tea house, and jardinieres, all common elements of a formal garden.

To the east on the lower terrace is the ITALIAN GARDEN. Its three formal pools are part of a design concept that dates back to the 16th century. These gardens have an architectural purity in which the plantings are secondary to the design. Nature is completely controlled and the gardens serve as an extension of the house. The outline of the three pools, grass areas and the paths are all part of a symmetrical design. The nearest pool contains the sacred lotus of Egypt. In the second are aquatic plants and in third, water lilies.

Down the broad stone stairway leading from the Italian Garden is a massive wisteria-covered PERGOLA. Even during the hottest days of summer, the fountains and deep shade make this a delightfully cool retreat.

In striking contrast to the terrace gardens is THE RAMBLE or SHRUB GARDEN which leads from the Italian Garden to the English Walled Garden. Olmsted used this design for "The Ramble" in Central Park to accommodate a steep incline with comfortable walks. Its winding gravel path is bordered by flowering shrubs, fine specimens of Japanese cut-leaf maples, azaleas, and dogwoods which provide a succession of color from late March to summer.

At the foot of The Ramble stands a stone wall behind which lies the four-acre English Walled Garden. Described as "the finest English garden in America," the garden is maintained in the grand tradition of the old English private garden. It is a flower garden in the fullest sense, containing no statues or fountains. Like its counterparts in northern Europe and Great Britain, it is designed to trap sunshine, exclude cold wind and create a warmer climate. It also is consistent with Francis Bacon's opinion, contained in his *Essays* of 1625, that "The garden is best to be square." Within the garden walls are square pattern beds derived from the Elizabethan "knot work" gardens in which the flowers form a decorative tapestry.

These square beds are planted three times a year. Approximately 50,000 tulip bulbs, imported from Holland, are planted every fall. In May they are replaced with summer bedding plants: marigolds, blue and red salvia, dahlias, cannas, and zinnias. With the advent of fall, the annual flowers give way to multi-hued varieties of Chrysanthemums, which usually last until the first heavy frost.

Along the walls are espaliered fruit trees and ornamental shrubs growing flat against the stone. They are complemented by weeping cherries, double dogwoods, crab apples and other flowering trees. The extensive perennial borders that follow the wall produce a progression of blooms: daffodils and hyacinths in the spring; peonies, iris, day lilies, phlox, bleeding-heart, lythrium, and many others through the summer.

The lower half of the garden contains the ROSE GARDEN, featuring All-American Rose Selections as well as over 3,000 roses of the finest varieties. Beyond it rises THE CONSERVATORY and its adjoining greenhouses. Rebuilt in 1957 consistent with Richard Morris Hunt's original plans, the Conservatory complex serves the same function it did in Vanderbilt's time: providing Biltmore House with cut flowers and plants and growing bedding plants for the estate's gardens.

The prominent central room contains the larger specimens such as palm trees, banana trees, schefflera and others which are used in Biltmore House. In the smaller adjacent rooms are displays of ferns, cacti, orchids, and other tropical plants.

THE BASS POND

Biltmore Estate is also blessed with an abundance of native plants. The most impressive showing of these can be found in the AZALEA GARDEN which contains the world's most complete collection of native azaleas. These plants were assembled by Chauncy Delos Beadle, a Canadian horticulturist, who came to work at Biltmore under Frederick Law Olmsted in 1890. He eventually became the Superintendent of Biltmore Estate, a post he held for sixty years.

Together with several friends nicknamed "the Azalea Hunters," Beadle gathered specimens from New Hampshire to Florida, Michigan and Texas. In 1940 he gave his prized collection to Biltmore Estate. Interspersed among the native plants are many Asiatic and hybrid azaleas, fine metasequois and rare magnolias. The magnificent evergreens found throughout are reminders that this area was once a pinetum, a living collection of evergreens.

Below the Azalea Garden lies the BASS POND, home to Biltmore's gaggle of geese. A wooden boathouse and gazebo provide a secluded resting place at the garden's end. At the opposite end of the pond is a foot bridge that crosses a waterfall flowing into a romantic ravine of rocky pools and bubbling streams.

The FORESTS on the Estate hold a key place in the history of forestry and conservation in America. When one drives through the fine pine groves, it is difficult to realize that most were planted just before the beginning of this century. It is often assumed that Mr. Vanderbilt bought much of this land because it was rich woodland. Actually, the land east of the French Broad River was badly eroded, and the few remaining scrub trees had to be removed before the trees which form the present woodlands could be planted.

Mr. Vanderbilt employed Gifford Pinchot (1865-1946), the first trained American forester and later Governor of Pennsylvania, to plan and direct the renovations of these woodlands. The result was the first comprehensive forest plan in the Western Hemisphere. Supervision was needed for the extensive planting, the establishment of experimental areas and the lumbering of the large tracts west of the French Broad River. Dr. Carl A. Schenck (1868-1955) of Darmstadt, Germany, was brought over to be Chief Forester. Soon after this, J. Sterling Morton, U.S. Secretary of Agriculture, expressed the wish that more Americans had the interest in forestry held by Mr. Vanderbilt. He said, "Mr. Vanderbilt had more workers and a larger budget for his forestry projects than I have at my disposal for the whole Department of Agriculture."

Under Mr. Vanderbilt's sponsorship, Dr. Schenck founded the Biltmore School of Forestry in 1898, the first in America. Until its termination at the advent of World War I, this school trained many of the foresters who dominated the field in this country for many years. In the course of the work in the Mt. Pisgah section of the Estate, Dr. Schenck developed the "land use" concept of forestry and conservation. Several of the early experimental plots are still being studied by the U.S. Forestry Service, which keeps records of plant growth and thinning.

Today, the forests are being harvested on a sustained yield basis consistent with the best ideas of modern forestry, some of which were conceived and developed here.

THE FRUITS OF COMMERCE *by John LaFarge*

Continuing Mr. Vanderbilt's vision of a self-sustaining European estate, The Biltmore Company began research into growing wine grapes and producing premium wines on Biltmore Estate in the early 1970s. This research produced favorable results, commercial vineyards were established, and in 1979 the first Biltmore wines were offered for sale to our visitors.

In May of 1985, BILTMORE ESTATE WINERY officially opened to the public for tours and tastings. The 90,000 square foot facility is located in buildings originally designed by Richard Morris Hunt as part of the Biltmore Dairy operation. Today the expanded and renovated buildings not only house state-of-the art winemaking equipment, but also some of the finest examples of American stained glass. William H. Vanderbilt commissioned John LaFarge (1835-1910) to create an exquisite set of stained glass windows for his home in New York City. These windows from the William H. Vanderbilt house are featured in the Welcome Center, Tasting Room, and Retail Sales Area.

GRAPES READY FOR HARVEST

The story of winemaking begins in the WELCOME CENTER. Five display kiosks describe the role of winemaking in ancient civilizations and cultures and feature artifacts from these cultures. Hand-stenciled walls and Portuguese tiles complete the old-world flavor of this newest addition to Biltmore Estate.

The process of turning grapes into European-style wine begins in the VINEYARDS. Along the gentle slopes of the estate's west side are acres of Vitis vinifera, the European grape recognized for producing the best wine. White wines are made from Sauvignon Blanc, Chardonnay, Riesling, Gewurztraminer, and Chenin Blanc grapes; red wines from Pinot Noir, Gamay Beaujolais, Cabernet Sauvignon, Cabernet Franc and Merlot. Within the next decade, these plantings will be expanded to a total of 110 acres.

BILTMORE ESTATE WINEMASTER PHILIPPE JOURDAIN

Under the direction of French winemaster Philippe Jourdain, these vineyards are carefully tended throughout the year to produce rich, ripe clusters of grapes. In September the grapes are harvested and taken to the winery where they are pressed. At this point they are processed, depending on the wine desired.

The processing begins in the stainless steel tanks housed in the FERMENTATION ROOM. Through a series of chemical reactions under anaerobic (without oxygen) conditions, fermentation occurs. During the two weeks that follow, sugar existing in the grape juice is converted into alcohol and carbon dioxide. The more sugar that is converted to alcohol, the drier the wine.

Once fermentation is completed, the wine is ready for the next and probably most important step, aging. For white wines the aging time is relatively brief and done in the stainless steel tanks. Biltmore red wines are aged in fine-grained French and American oak barrels. These barrels are kept in the AGING ROOM in a controlled environment for up to three years or more, depending on the quality of wine desired.

When the wine is ready for bottling, it is taken to a fully automated BOTTLING ROOM. Bottles are placed on a conveyer, run through a cleaning process which first vacuums the bottles then injects gas to sterilize them. After they're cleaned, the bottles move into a sealed room where they're filled with wine which has been filtered a final time to ensure purity.

When full, the bottles pass through a corking machine and leave the sterile room. As the bottles continue on the bottling line, a machine places lead capsules over the tops. Finally they are labeled and packed for the consumer.

The bottling of Biltmore champagne is still done by hand and can be viewed twice a year in the CHAMPAGNE BOTTLING ROOM. The champagne is made using the "methode champenoise" which was developed in the 17th century by a Benedictine monk named Dom Pierre Perignon. It begins with a white wine made of Chardonnay or Pinot Noir grapes. After the initial fermentation, the white wine is placed in long neck bottles and the wine undergoes a second fermentation in the bottle. It is this fermentation that gives champagne its distinctive bubbles.

As the fermentation occurs, dead yeast cells collect in the bottle and must be removed. This is done through a process called riddling. The bottles are placed neck down in a riddling rack, like the ones on display in the CELLARS. The bottles are rotated regularly, forcing the dead cells to settle in the neck of the bottles. The bottles' necks are then placed in a zero degree Fahrenheit brine solution until an ice cap forms, trapping the sediment, or lees. The temporary cap is removed, the frozen sediment disgorged, and the bottle topped with a special mixture of wine and sugar to replace the lost contents. Finally, the familiar mushroom cork is added.

The true test of any wine is in the taste. Amid the beauty of the restored dairy complex, Biltmore wines are sampled in the TASTING ROOM. For those people wishing to purchase the wine of their choice, the RETAIL SALES AREA offers a complete selection of Biltmore wines, wine books, coolers, glasses, and accoutrements.

DEERPARK COURTYARD

DEERPARK Restaurant is part of a series of handsome outbuildings designed by architect Richard Morris Hunt in the 1890's for George Vanderbilt's farm operations. Originally a dairy barn, Deerpark has been renovated into a unique open-air restaurant in a beautiful pastoral setting. The historic architectural detailing of the half-timbered woodwork, pebble-dash plaster and decorative brickwork are reminiscent of a farm landscape of the previous century.

The name Deerpark is taken from the nearby area of the Estate which George Vanderbilt set aside as a deer preserve. Many of the great estates of America and Europe include deer parks. They provided protection for the deer and the sight of the herds grazing created a delightful effect on the landscape. Today, the descendants of the deer herds which were established by Mr. Vanderbilt still can be seen on the hills of Biltmore Estate.

APPENDIX

The following appendix contains an itemized listing of the contents of each room. The objects are categorized into "Furniture," "Paintings and Prints," and "Decorative Objects."

MAIN FLOOR

VESTIBULE, ENTRANCE HALL, & STAIRCASE HALL

FURNITURE:
Metal-based table with petrified wood top, French, 19th c.
Iron strong chest, Spanish, 17th c.
Elizabethan style carved humpback chest, English, 19th c.
Tooled-leather armchair, Spanish, 19th c.
Renaissance-style oak table, designed by R.M. Hunt, American, 19th c.
Tall case clock, J. Numan, Amsterdam, 18th c.
Spanish provincial side chairs and sofa, 18th c.
Renaissance-style lectern, American 19th c.
Three-legged octagon table, 19th c.
Brass-topped table with turned wooden base, 19th c.
Hat rack, late 19th or early 20th c.
Six wrought iron lamps, American, c. 1895

DECORATIVE OBJECTS:
Bust of Richard Morris Hunt, marble, by Mary Grant, English, c. 1895
Roger and Angelique on the Hippogriff, with flanking candelabras, bronze, Antoine-Louis Barye, French, 19th c. Barye (1796-1875) is one of a group of 19th c. European sculptors specializing in animal figures. The *Animaliers* emphasized realism in both themes of hunting and attacking, and in their musculature portrayals. R.M. Hunt, architect of Biltmore, introduced Barye's work to Mr. Vanderbilt on a trip to Europe. This was probably the inspiration for Mr. Vanderbilt's collection of *Animaliers* sculpture found throughout Biltmore House.
Reproduction Oriental carpet, late 20th c.
Elevator, Otis, late 19th c., original to construction of mansion

WINTER GARDEN

FURNITURE:
Bamboo and rattan furniture, Perret & Fils et Vibert, Paris, 19th c.

DECORATIVE OBJECTS:
Brass oil lamps, probably from India, 19th c.

Boy and Geese fountain, marble and bronze, 1893-95, by Karl Bitter (1867-1915). This sculpture was the first fountain of Karl Bitter's career.
Reproduction Oriental carpets, late 20th c.

BILLIARD ROOM

FURNITURE:
Rack, pool & billiard tables, American, 19th c.
Leather upholstered Knole-style settees, arm and side chairs, Morant & Co., London, 19th c.
Highback leather side chairs, Flemish, 19th c.
Sheraton-style table with lyre legs, American, 19th c.
Trestle table with column supports, French, 19th c.
Renaissance octagonal table, Italian, 17th c.
Late Renaissance-style carved oak cabinet, German, 19th c.
French provincial drop-front desk, 18th c.
Stamped leather chairs, Portuguese, 17th c.
Bookcase with drawers, 19th c.

PAINTINGS AND PRINTS:
Rosita by Ignacio Zuloaga y Zabaleta, Spanish, 19th c.
English sporting & theater prints; Landseer, Reynolds, Atkinson, & Stubbs

DECORATIVE OBJECTS:
Two blue & white jugs, Delft, Dutch, 19th c.
Two steins with pewter lids, Villeroy & Boch, German, 19th c.
Bronze lamp, 19th c.
Terrier, bronze, by P.J. Mene, Berlin, 19th c.
Wrought iron standing lamps, American, 19th c.
Globe, C.F. Weber Co. successors to A.H. Andrews & Co., Chicago, 19th c.
Balloon clock, James Robson, London, c. 1780
Firewood holder, wrought iron and cast iron, 19th c.
Fireplace set, wrought iron and brass, 19th c.
Candlesticks, wood, Biltmore Industries, American, c. 1910
Game-point counting instrument, 19th c.
Pipe stand, 19th c.
Two weft-wrapped carpets, E. Caucasus, Sumak tribe, 19th c.

BANQUET HALL

FURNITURE:
Banquet table, by R.M. Hunt, American, 19th c.
Throne chairs, designed by R.M. Hunt, carved by Karl Bitter, American, 19th c.
67 arm and side chairs, Italian, 19th c.

TAPESTRIES:
Vulcan & Venus Tapestries, Flemish, 16th c.

Information on the tapestries is based on two articles by Mrs. Ella S. Siple, of the Cincinnati Museum of Art, which appeared in the *Burlington Magazine*, Vol. 73, Nov. 1938, pp 212-221 & Vol. 74 June 1939, pp 268-279.

The story told in the Venus and Vulcan tapestries is found in Ovid. *The Metamorphosis* was probably the source for the Biltmore House version. The following are the subjects represented and free translation of the Latin inscriptions:

No 1, on the right of the wall facing the entrance, is *THE DANCE:* three dancing figures are in the center. In the left foreground are Mars and Venus in amorous embrace. In the distance at the left is a castle, in which we see Vulcan at his forge. Translation of the Latin: "The impatient Venus put aside all sense of shame, but wrath and the frenzy of rage, ever to be associated with Mars, make Vulcan choke and writhe. Ordinarily, moderate loves do not fall to pieces; he who scorns the lessons of life as his limit will pass his years in sorrow and loathing, bereft of reason."

No. 2, on the left of the fireplace, is *VULCAN FORGING AND SPREADING THE NET:* The interior of Vulcan's palace is in the Flemish Renaissance style. At the left, Vulcan is at his anvil and through an open doorway are his assistants at the forge. At the right Vulcan appears again spreading the net over the bed of Venus. He is assisted by two elderly female servants, one of whom represents Jealousy. Translation of the Latin: "The mournful Vulcan thinks of his craft; he fashions a delicate copper net and, stretching this over the couch, he fits it closely so that both shall be caught. Love and beauty are treacherous phantoms, by which are ensnared the minds of fools, whom never-fading passion, though thrice indulged, cannot sate."

No. 3, in the center of the wall, is *THE COMPLAINT TO JUPITER:* Vulcan stands in the right foreground with arms raised toward heaven. He calls upon the other gods, three of whom—Jupiter, Diana and Pallas—appear in the clouds of the upper right. Translation of the Latin: "Mars and Venus, captured, are held by the chains and the artificer asks the gods to look upon them: Diana and Pallas modestly scorn to look upon their sin. Pleasure always gives rise to quarrels, it spreads and is fostered by a deceitful flame; wise chastity teaches how to beware the chains of wickedness."

No. 4, on the right of the fireplace, is *THE ASSEMBLAGE OF THE GODS:* In the foreground, a number of gods and goddesses, including Jupiter are pointing towards Vulcan's palace in the middle distance. There they see Venus and Mars embracing. Translation of the Latin: "When the chamber which should have been concealed lay open and the disgrace was revealed, a laugh rang out; many of the gods were silently yearning to be caught in such a position. The pure set store by faithful marriage beds and Venus does not desert the begetting of offspring; a steadfast love has charms for those in wedlock and for those who always observe con-tinence in their passion."

No. 5, on the right of the entrance, is *NEPTUNE INTER-CEDING FOR THE LOVERS:* In another room in Vulcan's pal-ace, he sits disconsolate on his throne. In front of him is Neptune with his trident and Cupid. At the left are the Three Graces in attitudes of despair and above them is an opening through which may be seen Venus and Mars. A small figure (Vulcan?) removes the net from the bed. Trans-lation of the Latin: "The Graces plead through the lips of Neptune, and Cupid asks that he loose the bond; by their entreaties the wicked husband is warned, he frees them both. All respect the pact of peace, the Graces again are favorable to the lovers and the dark rumors of suspicion quit the established bed."

The Venus and Vulcan series is one of the two best known of the 16th Century Flemish design; the other is Raphael's Acts of the Apostles. Both were copied with vari-ations at Mortlake and Lambeth in the 17th Century. First written mention of the Biltmore House set was in 1876, in a catalogue: *Cinquieme Exposition, Union Centrale des Beaux-Arts Appliques a l'Industries,* and in the *Gazette des Beaux-Arts,* Paris. In the latter, one Alfred Darcel tells how he found them rolled up in the gardenmeuble of the Chateau de la Roche-Guyon. They must have come on the market soon thereafter; in 1885 a M. Jourdain owned them. In 1887 Mr. Vanderbilt bought them. They are believed to have been woven in Brussels either shortly before 1547, or at any rate before 1553. Mrs. Siple writes: "The more one studies the designs the more one is convinced that they were the work of some Flemish Raphael, some northern artist or artists in close touch with Italian painting, either directly or through engraved reproductions. Both the landscapes and the archi-tecture are in the accepted Flemish style. Many of the figure motives, however, are copies or adapted from earlier Italian designs...The costumes of the leading characters are consis-tent throughout, and the figure designs lean heavily on engravings by Marcantonio Raimondi, or on the Raphael drawings from which Marcantonio worked...In all proba-bility there were more than five in the original set, complet-ing the story. It is possible that some scenes from the original Flemish series have come down to us only in Mortlake versions.

FLAGS:
The state flags & mottoes are listed clockwise from the right of the fireplace
Rhode Island, "Hope"
Maryland, "Deeds are male, words female"
New Hampshire, rising sun & ship building
Massachusetts, "Come over and help us"
Pennsylvania, "Virtue, Liberty and Independence"
New Jersey, "Liberty and Prosperity"
Georgia, red stripes with seal on blue ground
   "don't Tread on Me," Revolutionary War Flag

South Carolina, "Ready with our hearts and deeds"
"Liberty or Death," Revolutionary War Flag
Virginia, "So may all tyrants perish"
New York, "Excelsior"
Connecticut, white flag with grapevines
Delaware, "Liberty and Independence"
North Carolina, "To be rather than to seem "
Pennants above fireplace represent countries in power
    when Columbus discovered America.
Biltmore Service Flag

DECORATIVE OBJECTS:
Brass and copper vessels, Dutch, Spanish & French, 18th
    and 19th c.
Armor, 15th to 19th c., clockwise form immediate left
Halberds, broadswords, helmet, coat of mail
Halberds, two-handed broadswords, helmet, shield
Breastplate, helmet, lances, double-edged swords
Lances, headsman's axe, epaulliere, breastplate
Two corridor carpets, Persian, Khorassan area, 19th c.
Corridor carpet, Persian, Bijar area, 19th c.

BREAKFAST ROOM

FURNITURE:
Dining table, American, c. 1865
Gilt side chairs and daybeds, Italian, 19th c.
Trestle table with column supports, 19th c.
Draw table with satyr legs, Italian, 16th c.
Table with melon-bulb legs, Italian, 19th c.
Brass display cabinet, American, 19th c.

PAINTINGS:
Beginning above the display case, clockwise around the
    room, the family portraits are;
William H. Vanderbilt, by Jared B. Flagg (1820-1899), c.
    1877
Sophia (Mrs. Cornelius) Vanderbilt, George Vanderbilt's
    grandmother, artist unknown, n.d.
Commodore Cornelius Vanderbilt as a Young Man, George
    Vanderbilt's grandfather, by Charles Loring Elliot
    (1812-1868), American, c. 1839
Maria Louisa (Mrs. William) Vanderbilt, George
    Vanderbilt's mother, by George A. Baker (1821-1880),
    n.d.
Jacob Hand Vanderbilt, by Charles Loring Elliot, n.d.
Unknown Gentleman, artist unknown, n.d.
Maria Louisa (Mrs. William) Vanderbilt as a young woman,
    artist unknown, n.d.
Commodore Cornelius Vanderbilt, by Jared B. Flagg, c.
    1876

DECORATIVE OBJECTS:
Ivory figurines, European, 19th c.

Vanderbilt dinnerware, Minton & Spode, English, early
    20th c.
Vanderbilt crystal, Baccarat, French, and Webb, English,
    19th c.
Bird pattern dessert dishes, Minton, English, 19th c.
Moonlight lustreware in shell pattern, Wedgwood, English,
    19th c.
Oriental-motif dishes, Royal Worcester, English, late 19th c.
Pastoral couples, Chelsea mark, French, 19th c.
Meissen candlesticks, German, 18th c.
Pair of silver plated candlesticks, Sheffield, English, 19th c.
Three porcelain serving pieces with hand-painted decora-
    tion, 19th c.
Lanterns, Italian, 18th c.
Reproduction flatware, American, 20th c.
Carpet, Persian, Joshegan or Shiraz area, 19th c.

SALON

FURNITURE:
Louis XV-style settee & chairs, French, 19th c.
Pembroke table, English, 19th c.
Paper mache table with mother-of-pearl inlay and gilding,
    French, 19th c.
Petit point folding screen, French, 19th c.
Louis XV style double desk, French, 19th c.
Two Sheraton-style chairs, English, 19th c.
Rococo bombé commode decorated with floral and geomet-
    ric inlay, Dutch, 18th c.
Pembroke table with claw feet, English, 19th c.
Napoleon's game table, French, 19th c.
Gothic style table, American, 19th c.

PRINTS:
Engravings by Albrecht Dürer, German, 16th c. A. Dürer
    was the most influential northern European artist to
    bring Renaissance art from Italy to the rest of Europe.
    These exquisitely detailed drawings were carefully
    carved onto woodblocks and then printed onto paper.
    Dürer's prints included religious, mythological and
    genre themes.
Portrait prints by R. Nanteuil, French, 17th c.
Chateaux prints by O. deRochebrune, French, 19th c.

DECORATIVE OBJECTS:
Ivory chess set, Chinese, 19th c.
Bust of Napoleon, marble, 19th c.
Cardinal Richelieu's embroidered hangings, French,
    17th c.
Faience letter box, French, 19th. c.
Faience candlesticks, French, 19th c.
Faience desk set, J. Borrelly, French, 1749
Pair of bronze candlesticks, by A.L. Barye, French, 19th c.

Bust, *A. Miner*, bronze, by Constantin Emile Meunier (1831-1905), Brussels, 19th c.

Bust of Stevedore, inscribed "Anvers", by Constantin Emile Meunier (1831-1905), Belgian, 19th c. Both busts have the foundry mark: *Fondu par verbetst pour Atelier Constantin Meunier, Bruxelles.*

Bust, unknown female, bronze, French, 19th c.

Lamp, American, 19th c.

Pair of tall lamps, 19th c.

Carpet, Persian, Sarabend area, 19th c.

Carpet, Persian, Ferrehan area, 19th c.

WINTER GARDEN CORRIDOR

FURNITURE:

Brass-studded hobnail chest, Spanish, 16th c.

Renaissance-style oak chest with cushion, American, 19th c.

Upholstered sofas, American, 19th c.

Renaissance torcheres, probably Italian, 17th c.

Italian *dantesca*-style chairs, Biltmore Furniture Conservation Shop, 1980

DECORATIVE OBJECTS:

Plaster copies of frieze metopes from the Parthenon, by Eugene Arrondelle, French, 19th c.

MUSIC ROOM

FURNITURE:

Baroque-style settee & armchairs, Italian, 19th c.

Monastery table, style of the 17th c.

Gothic-style credenza, French, 19th c.

Music stand, carved and gilded, 18th c.

Octagon table with lion legs, Italian, 19th c.

Renaissance-style armchairs, Italian, 19th c.

Chest on stand, late Renaissance-style Italian, 19th c.

Inlaid sideboard, late Gothic-style, German, 19th c.

Steinway piano, American, early 20th c.

Carved side chair with upholstered seat, Spanish, 19th c.

PRINTS:

Triumphal Arch of Maximillian, A. Dürer, German, 1515

DECORATIVE OBJECTS:

Sacrificial vessel, Chinese, Chou Dynasty (1027 to 221 B.C.)

Vessel, Chinese, Han Dynasty (206 B.C. to 220 A.D.)

Meissen Apostle with accompanying candlesticks, by J. Kändler, German, 18th c.

Gilt statue, St. John, French, 18th c.

Gilt statue, St. Peter, French, 18th c.

Two bronze figures of water gods, unsigned, French, 19th c.

Three bronze parrots, by A.L. Barye, French, 19th c.

Wrought iron torcheres, American 19th c.

Four wooden floor lamps, Biltmore Furniture Conservation Shop, 1976

Pair of iron candelabra, 17th c.

Two carpets, Persian, Khorassan area, 19th c.

Carpet, Persian, Tabriz area, 19th c.

GALLERY

FURNITURE:

Semicircular cabinet, Italian, 17th c.

Walnut stool, Italian, 19th c.

Ebony cabinet on stand with interior painted scenes, Flemish, 17th c.

Two gateleg tables, American, early 20th c., probably produced by Biltmore Industries, Asheville

Vargueno (desk/curio cabinet), Spanish, c. 1600. This elaborate piece of furniture includes examples of a wide variety of decorative elements practiced in Spain at the end of the 16th c. Turned and inlaid ivory, gilding, painting, and iron work are all incorporated into both the *taquillion* (base) and the *vargueno* (desk).

Semi-circular fold-top table, English, early 17th c.

Three gothic-style tables, German, 19th c.

Gothic-style chest incorporating 15th/16th c. panels, French, 19th c.

Five gothic-style credenzas (cupboards), French, 19th c. These credenzas incorporate panels and doors dating to late 15th c., but the major portions of the pieces were constructed in the 19th c.

Two carved tables, Italian, 19th c.

Upholstered sofas and chairs, English, 19th c.

Renaissance-style carved table, 19th c.

Two stamped leather side chairs, Spanish, 19th c.

PAINTINGS:

Portrait, hanging to left of door into library, Maria Louisa (Mrs. William) Vanderbilt, by John Singer Sargent, c. 1895

Portrait, hanging above door into library, Mr. George Vanderbilt, by John Singer Sargent, American, c. 1900

Portrait, hanging to the right of the door into library, Edith (Mrs. George) Vanderbilt, by Giovanni Boldini, Italian, c. 1900

DECORATIVE OBJECTS:

Two majolica vases made into lamps, 19th c.

Basket clock, by E. Card, London, England, late 17th/early 18th c.

Inverted bell clock, by E. Burgis, London, England, late 17th/early 18th c.

Figured brass and copper bowl with lid, 19th c.

Brass collection plate, 19th c.

Icon of Madonna and Child, Russian, 1810

Family photographs

Figure of cat climbing into kettle, 19th c.

Bronze bust, *George Washington*, after-cast by fonduer F. Barbedienne after original by Jean-Antoine Houdon (1741-1828), French, 19th c.

Bronze bust, *Benjamin Franklin*, after-cast by fonduer F. Barbedienne after original by Jean-Antoine Houdon (1741-1828), French, 19th c.

Bronze stag, by A.L. Bayre, French, 19th c.

Bronze of Hercules and Antaeus, French, 19th c.

Bronze candelabras, French, 19th c.

Four large Satsuma vases, Japanese, 19th c.

Bronze dromedary with rider, by A.L. Barye, French, 19th c.

Bronze dromedary, by A.L. Barye, French, 19th c.

Two bronze candelabras, by A.L. Barye, French, 19th c.

Glass fire screen, enameled leaded glass with rosewood frame, American, c. 1895. This firescreen was presented to R.M. Hunt, Biltmore House architect, by the workmen involved in construction of the mansion.

Four wrought iron floor lamps with turtle bases, American, c. 1895

Pair of candlesticks, bronze, French, 19th c.

Small wooden inlaid box, Syrian, early 20th c.

Three carpets, Persian, Sarabend area, 19th c.

Carpet, Persian, Lori Tribe, 19th c.

TAPESTRIES:

The Triumph of Virtue over Vice tapestries

No. 1, *THE TRIUMPH OF PRUDENCE.* Translation of Latin inscription: "Moderation restrains the impulses of the spirit and with her measure curbs you, Pluto, Lyeus (Bacchus), Venus."

In the center is the wreath-crowned Prudence on her wheeled throne inscribed *Prudenum.* She holds a sceptre, mirror and serpent.

No. 2, *THE TRIUMPH OF FAITH.* Translation of Latin inscription: "Holy Faith trusts in the divine word and devotes herself wholly to God with dutiful reverence."

Christian Faith triumphant is seated on a throne on wheels, drawn by animals symbolic of the Evangelists. She is show in aureole, holds a cross and church in one hand, a chalice and host in the other, Inri, above cross, stands for Jesus of Nazareth, King of Jews. Three crowned figures in clouds above, each holding an orb, represent the Trinity.

No. 3, *THE TRIUMPH OF CHARITY.* Translation of the Latin inscription: "He who loves the powers of heaven with all his heart, performs all the duties which piety imposes."

Charitas, Charity, enthroned in her chariot, holds a red heart and points toward the face of Christ, from which radiate rays of light. In front of her is the symbol of redemption through suffering frequently found in the religious art of the time, a pelican plucking out its vitals to feed its young.

LIBRARY

FURNITURE:

Settees, arm and side chairs, Italian, 19th c.

Elaborate carved table, Italian, 19th c.

Slant-front book display rack, American, 19th c.

Jacobean-style bookbinding press, English, 19th c.

Fire bench, bronze, American, 19th c.

Pair of two-tiered tables, probably by Biltmore Industries, American, c. 1910

PAINTING:

The Chariot of Aurora, Italian, 18th c. Ceiling painting by Giovanni Antonio Pelligrini (1675-1741), brought to Biltmore House from the Pisani Palace in Venice, Italy, by George Vanderbilt.

DECORATIVE OBJECTS:

Lectern with crowned eagle, carved and gilded, German, 18th c.

Pair of bronze incense burners with figures, 19th c.

Three goldfish bowls, Chinese, Ming Dynasty (1368-1644)

Two blue and white porcelain oil lamps, Chinese, 19th c.

Globe, Malby's Terrestrial Globe, Edward Stanford Geographical Publisher, London, 1899

Bronze bust of George Vanderbilt, by Mary Grant, English, 1900

Two porcelain urns, Naples mark, 19th c.

Miniatures of master painters, Italian, 19th c. The ten painters depicted worked during the 15th, 16th and 17th c.

Document repository, Japanese, 18th

Plaster busts of French nobles and philosophers, French, 19th c. Left to right: Cardinal Mazarin, Cornelle, Moliere, Montaigne, Voltaire, Racine, and Cardinal Richelieu

Library magnifying glasses, walnut, 19th c.

Baroque clock with gilded putti and satyrs, Italian, mid-18th c.

Four brass lamps on marble bases, American, late 19th c.

Eight-arm brass candelabra, French, 18th c.

Three rolling step ladders, 19th c.

Pair of small three-legged chairs, probably American, early 20th c.

Tapestry, possibly a scene from the life of Alexander the Great, French, 17th c.

Corridor carpet, Persian, Karahagh, 19th c.

Carpet, Persian, Herat area, 19th c.

Runner, Caucasian, Kuba, 19th c.

STAIRWAY LANDINGS

Gothic tapestry, French or Flemish, 15th c.

Bronze bust, by A.C. Belleuse, French, 19th c.

Marble bust of Julius Caesar, 19th c.
Marble bust of Augustus Caesar, 19th c.
Louis XV cabinet with pendulum clock, French, 18th c.
Gothic-style pedestal, probably French, 19th c.
Italian *dantesca*-style chairs, Biltmore Furniture Conservation Shop, 1980

LOUIS XVI ROOM

FURNITURE:
Inlaid bed with brass mounts, French, 18th c.
Louis XVI-style chaise and four side chairs, gilded, French, 19th c.
Louis XVI roll-top desk with brass mounts, French, 19th c.
Pair of Louis XVI console tables, gilded, French, 19th c.
Louis XVI night table, French 18th c.
Parquetry night table, French, early 19th c.
Kidney-shaped parquetry table, French, 18th c.
Gilded floor mirror, French, 19th c.

PRINTS:
French school of portraiture including Drevet, Muller, 19th c.

DECORATIVE OBJECTS:
Bust of Dauphin, Louis XVII, marble, French, 19th c.
Three-arm candelabra, unglazed porcelain, Sevres, French, 18th c.
Faience desk set, by J. Pfau, French, 18th c.
Ruby-cut glass decanters and covered dish, 19th c.
Vases made into lamps, French, 19th c.
Cartel clock, Louis Jouard, Paris, mid-18th c.
Letter opener, French, 19th c.
Desk accessory/candlestick, French, 18th c.
Pair of candelabra
Three piece garniture set: two vases and ginger jar, armorial-style, Chinese, 19th c.
Aubusson carpets, French, 19th c.

SECOND FLOOR LIVING HALL

FURNITURE:
Three baroque-style armchairs, Italian, 19th c.
Gilded cassone (chest), Italian, 17th c., with pedimental mirror, Italian, 19th c.
Painted leather coffer chest with brass straps and lock, Italian, 19th c.
Boulle-style desk with pewter and brass inlay, French, 19th c.
Rococo armchair with claw & ball feet, Flemish, 18th c.
Two Jacobean-style armchairs with scroll feet, style of 17th c., English, 19th c.
Queen Anne-style settee, English, 19th c.

Queen Anne-style wing chair, style of 17th c., English, 19th c.
Barrel-back chair, 19th c.
Settee, 19th c.
Pedestal table, style of 17th c.
Four gateleg tables, 19th c.
Gothic-style chest, 19th c.
Gothic-style pedestal, 19th c.
Travel chest with ivory, mother-of-pearl, brass and enamel inlay, probably Spanish, 19th c.; travel chest stand, American, early 20th c.
Chest on stand, Jacobean, English, 17th c.

PAINTINGS:
Richard M. Hunt, by John Singer Sargent, American, 1895
Frederick L. Olmsted, by John Singer Sargent, American, 1895
The Waltz, by Anders Zorn, Swedish, (1860-1920)
The dancer in the forefront is a self-portrait of the artist. Zorn exhibited this painting at the Columbia Exposition in Chicago, 1893, where it was purchased by Mr. Vanderbilt.
William H. Vanderbilt family, by Seymour Guy, American, 1873. Guy was born in England in 1824 and studied under Butterworth and Ambrose Jerome. He settled in New York in 1854.
Painting of W.H. Vanderbilt family yacht, artist unknown, late 19th/early 20th c.
Genre painting, by E.J. Verboeckhoven, Dutch, 1851

DECORATIVE OBJECTS:
Balloon clock, by Marriot, London, last quarter of the 18th c.
Boulle-style desk set, French, 19th c.
Tusk thermometer, 19th c.
Photographs of Vanderbilt family members
Poker set, late 19th/early 20th c.
Mah Jong set, Hong Kong, 19th c.
Roulette wheel, 19th c.
Mother-of-pearl poker chips, Tiffany & Co., American, 19th c.
Bronze figure of a female peasant, by Valligren, 1893
Statue, Commodore Cornelius Vanderbilt, bronze, American, 19th c. This statue is a small version of the larger-than-life-size original that stands in front of Grand Central Station, New York City
Pair of porcelain parrots on bronze mounts, 19th c.
Statue, *Messonier*, bronze, by Gemilo, French, 19th c.
Statue, *Goddess of Mercy*, porcelain, Chinese, 18th c.
Satsuma incense burner with peacock, Japanese, 19th c., displayed in gilded wall case, French, 18th c.
Satsuma ewer with dragon, Japanese, 19th c., displayed in gilded wall case, French, 18th c.
Statue clock with elephant and Chinese figure, probably Jappy Brothers, French, c. 1870.
Four blue porcelain vases, Chinese, 19th c.

Oil lamp made from a vase, 19th c.
Books, 19th c.
Magazines, early 20th c.
Carpet, Persian, Herat area, 19th c.
Carpet, Persian, 19th c.
Silk carpet, Persian, Tabriz area, 19th c.

SECOND FLOOR CORRIDOR

FURNITURE:
Two floral inlaid cabinet-on-stands, Dutch, 19th c.
Two cacqueteuse chairs, French, 16th c.
Marble-topped bombé commode with hairy claw feet, Italian, 18th c.
Two inlaid armchairs with rush seats, German, style of the 17th c.
Pair of tables with scrolled stretcher, Spanish, 19th c.
Gothic-style credenza, American, 19th c.
Three sidechairs with stamped leather seats and backs, Flemish, 18th c.
Italian *dantesca*-style chair, Biltmore Furniture Conservation Shop, 1987

PAINTINGS & PRINTS:
Engravings by 18th c. French and English artists: Woollett, Strange, Mason, Canot, Vivare, and Francois
The Christening, by Joseph Villegas, Spanish, 1880. This study was in the William H. Vanderbilt collection. The whereabouts of the final version is unknown.

DECORATIVE OBJECTS:
Vase with ormolu fittings, Chinese, 18th c.
Bronze candelabra, by August Nicholas Cain (1821-1904), French, late 19th c.
Japanese curios, netsukes, daggers, boxes, and tea caddies, 18th and 19th c. The objects were bought by Mr. Vanderbilt on his visit to Japan in 1892. The extensive collection of Oriental objects collected by Mr. Vanderbilt also includes swords, vases, and figurines, many of which can be seen on display throughout Biltmore House.
Bronze bust of Moliere, French, 19th c.
Marble bust of Demosthenes, Wedgwood & Bentley, 19th c.
Terra-cotta bust of a woman, French, 19th c.
Bust of Diana, bronze, n.d.

SOUTH BEDROOM,
MR. VANDERBILT'S ROOM

FURNITURE:
Bed with tester, Spanish, 17th c.
Settee, chaise, 6 chairs, and 2 armchairs, American, 19th c. Probably designed by R.M. Hunt and made by Baumgarten & Co. in New York.

Dressing/writing table with pier glass, American, c. 1894. Designed by R.M. Hunt and made by Baumgarten & Co. in New York.
Large table, twist legs, style of 17th c., Portuguese, 19th c.
Small table, twist legs, style of 17th c., Portuguese, 19th c.
Chest-on-chest, Italian, 19th c.
Two chests with figured handles, Spanish, 17th c.
Gilt mirror with crown, Spanish, 17th c.
Wall stand, Spanish, 17th c.
Three carved ebony stands, East Indian, 19th c.
Cabinet with textile, 17th c.

PRINTS:
Engravings by 16th and 17th c. artists of Germany, Holland, and Flanders: Visscher, Aldegrever, Wierex, and others

DECORATIVE OBJECTS:
Two brass candelabra, Italian, 19th c.
Boulle-style desk set, French, 18th c.
Inverted basket clock, French, 19th c.
Double hourglass, 19th c.
Two beaten bronze ewers, Spanish, 19th c.
Wood urn, East Indian, 19th c.
Hunting dogs with pheasant, signed "P.J. Mêne 1847"
Bronze eagle holding a heron, by A.L. Bayre, French, 19th c.
Bronze figure of Mercury, inscribed "AD", 19th c.
Bronze figure of Spartacus, inscribed "Foyetier 1832", French, 19th c.
Candelabra with coat of arms, Danish, 19th c.
Plaster friezes, busts, & urns; Eugene Arrondelle, French, 19th c.
Brass picture frame with cover, Tiffany & Co., American, late 19th c.
Pair of brass candelabra, possibly Indian, 19th c.
Carpet, Turkestan, Ersari tribe, 19th c.
Carpet, Persian, Sarab area, 19th c.

OAK SITTING ROOM

FURNITURE:
Ebony cabinet on stand, architectural interior, elaborate carved decoration, Antwerp, 17th c.
Ebony wardrobe, painted panels, German, 17th c.
Oak cupboard, German, style of the 16th c.
Inlaid kneehole desk, Spanish, 18th c.
Two chests, inlaid landscapes, Italian, 15th c.
Draw-top table, English, style of 17th c.
Renaissance-style walnut table, 19th c.
Ebony and ivory display cabinet, American, 19th c.
Carved side chairs with upholstered seats, 19th c.
Draw-top table, probably designed by R.M. Hunt, American, c. 1895.

PAINTINGS:

Left: Mrs. Benjamin Kissam, by John Singer Sargent, c. 1900
Right: Virginia Purdy Barker (Mrs. Walter) Bacon, by John
  Singer Sargent, 1896

DECORATIVE OBJECTS:

Blue & white garniture set: two vases & covered urn,
  French, 19th c.
Brass and copper wine coolers on lion's feet, 19th c. adapta-
  tions of an earlier piece. Wine coolers in the 17th and
  18th centuries were utilized at formal banquets. This
  pair was probably decorative rather than functional.
Clock with bronze figures, French, 19th c.
Two ivory-colored vases, Chinese, 18th c.
Delft urn, Holland, 19th c.
Covered urn, China, 19th c.
Two lacquer figures, Japanese, 19th c.
Four ceramic musicians, Japanese, 19th c.
Three vases, blue & white, Chinese, 19th c.
Coffee & tea service, floral pattern, Sevre, French, 1888
Upholstered mirrors, 19th c.
Tea set, rose & white, 19th c.
Walking Tiger, by A.L. Barye, French, c. 1865
Two bronze tigers, by A.L. Barye, French, 19th c.
Walking Lion, by A.L. Barye, French, c. 1865
Bronze man with a glass blowing pipe, by C. Meunier,
  French, 19th c.
Hammerman, bronze, by c. Meunier, French, 19th c.
The Iron Worker, bronze, by C. Meunier, French, 19th c.
Pair of bronze candlesticks in form of oil lamp, probably
  French, 19th c.
Pair of blue and white candlesticks, Danish, 19th c.
Two Ensi carpets, Turkestan, Tekke tribe, 19th c.
Carpet, Persian, Sarab area, 19th c.

NORTH BEDROOM,
MRS. VANDERBILT'S ROOM

FURNITURE:

Bed with canopy, American, 19th c.
Louis XV-style chairs & chaise lounge, French, 19th c.
Dressing table with mirror, English, 19th c.
Boulle-style table, English, 19th c.
Louis XV slant-top desk, French and Dutch, 18th c.
Two Louis XV commodes with marble tops, French, 18th c.
Pier glass, Louis XV-style, American, 19th c.
Two Directoire night tables, French, 19th c.
Cushions, 19th c.

PRINTS:

Nineteenth century engravings by Schmidt, Drevet, Roger,
  and Wille

DECORATIVE OBJECTS:

Brass figured candlesticks, French, 19th c.

Five silver filigree toilet bottles, French, 19th c.
Small painted and gilded urn, German, 19th c.
Three Porcelain figured candlesticks, Naples, 19th c.
Three majolica urns, Italian, 19th c.
Porcelain desk set, French & Dutch, 18th c.
Earthenware wine jug, Spanish, 19th c.
Porcelain elephant, English, 19th c.
Michel mantel clock, porcelain & brass, French, 18th c.
Savonnerie carpets, French, 19th c.
Small urn, German, late 19th c.
Compote, porcelain, Dresden, 19th c.

MRS. VANDERBILT'S BATH and
DRESSING AREA

FURNITURE:

Marble-topped side cabinet, English, 19th c.
Two towel racks, English, 19th c.
Regency side chair, English, 19th c.

DECORATIVE OBJECTS:

Porcelain toilet set, Minton and Spode, French, 19th c.
Ivory comb and brushes, 19th c.
Linens, French and American, 19th c.
Clothing accessories, late 19th/early 20th c.
Hat boxes, modern reproductions
Blankets, late 19th c.

MRS. VANDERBILT'S
LADYSMAID'S ROOM

Bed with carved decoration, late 19th c.
Dresser with mirror, late 19th c.
Wardrobe, oak, late 19th c.
Side chair with cane seat, Jacob, English, 19th c.
Counterpane bedspread, American, late 19th c.
Footstool, 19th c.
Oil lamp
Pair of porcelain figurines, Dutch, late 19th c.
Oil painting, landscape scene, probably on Biltmore Estate,
  Gerard Barry, American, early 20th c.
Pitcher and bowl, Minton, English, late 19th c.
Marble inlaid box, late 19th c.
Dresser scarf, late 19th c.
2 braided rugs, modern reproductions

SEWING ROOM

Wardrobe, oak, late 19th c.
Work table, oak, late 19th c.
Two chairs, 19th c.
Singer treadle sewing machine, early 20th c.
Dresser with mirror, chestnut, late 19th c.

Sewing accessories, modern reproductions of 19th c. objects
Wrought iron lamp, late 19th/early 20th c.
Wood stove, Ashley Automatic Woodstove Company, Columbia, South Carolina, early 20th c.
Ironing board, late 19th/early 20th c.

HALL CABINETS
Bed linens, late 19th c.
Fabric and related sewing accessories

MAIDS' SITTING ROOM

Pair of carved armchairs, rosewood, Roccoco revival, American, c. 1860.
Two leather armchairs, 19th c.
Drop-leaf table, 19th c.
Foot stool, 19th c.
Folding table, 19th c.
Table, chestnut, late 19th c.
Bookcase, Biltmore Industries, American, early 20th c.
Mortar and pestle, 20th c.
Book ends, Tryon Toy Co., American, c. 1920
Pewter tea pot, French, 19th c.
Tea set, Aynsley, English, 19th c.
Dog, 19th c.
Lamp, 19th c.
Dresser scarves, late 19th/early 20th c.
Photograph of Martha Laube, ladysmaid to Cornelia and Edith Vanderbilt, 1912-1915. Photo courtesy of Babette Schmaus.
Waste basket, late 19th/early 20th c.
Carpet, Chedor, Persian, 19th c.

HALLWAY

Side table, mahogany, English, 19th c.
Marble-topped table, rosewood, mid-19th c.
Two floor lamps, modern reproductions
Prints

THIRD FLOOR LIVING HALL

FURNITURE:
Piano, Wm. Knabe & Co., American, early 20th c.
Three glass-fronted cabinets, American, late 19th c. These cabinets came from William H. Vanderbilt's house on Fifth Avenue in New York City.
Side table, late 19th c.
Three inlaid armchairs with rush seats, German, style of the 17th c.
Pair of arm chairs with Aubusson upholstery, probably French, 19th c.
Oval inlaid tea table, Biltmore Industries, American, early 20th c.

Side cabinet with carved and fluted decoration, 17th c.
Pair of carved armchairs with stamped leather upholstery, probably English, 19th c.
Upholstered stool, 19th c.
Pair of highback side chairs with stamped leather upholstery, probably English, 17th c.
Drop leaf table, 19th c.
Six carved side chairs with upholstered seats, Italian, 19th c.
Sofa with two matching upholstered chairs, 19th c.
Two-tiered end table, 19th c.
Table, oak, American, late 19th c.
Inlaid side chair with leather seat, 18th c.
Folding side table, 19th c.
Small table with marble inset top, 19th c.
Pair of heavily carved armchairs, 19th c.

PAINTINGS AND PRINTS:
Portrait of Edith (Mrs. George) Vanderbilt, by James McNeill Whistler, American, c. 1900
Prints by James McNeill Whistler, Axel Haig, Sir Joshua Reynolds, G. Kneller, J.J. Hoppner, Van Dyck, and George Romney

DECORATIVE OBJECTS:
Set of eight monkey bandsmen, porcelain, Meissen, German, 19th c.
Stone sculpture, inscribed "Rosset," 19th c.
Hamlet, unglazed porcelain, 19th c.
Bust of a man, porcelain, 19th c.
Stuffed hawk, late 19th/early 20th c.
Books, 19th/early 20th c.
Pair of blue and white candlesticks, porcelain, 19th c.
Blue and white standing picture frame, porcelain, Delft, Dutch, 19th c.
Table ornament/candlestick, marble and brass, 19th c.
Pair of wooden candlesticks, probably Biltmore Industries, Asheville, American, c. 1905
Assorted Vanderbilt family photographs in reproduction frames
Pair of garnet wine glasses, late 19th c.
Pair of embroidered linens, with "MLV" monogram for Maria Louisa Vanderbilt, mother of G.V. Vanderbilt, late 19th c.
Bronze female bust, French, 19th c.
Bronze nude female, French, 19th c.
Bronze nude boy, French, 19th c.
Bronze female bust, French, 19th c.
Miniature bronze bust, French, 19th c.
Bronze kneeling woman, French, 19th c.
Bronze turtles, inscribed with Oriental mark, 19th c.
Covered bowl, 19th c.
Lamp made from vase, 19th c.
Carved stool, Biltmore Industries, Asheville, American, c. 1905

Pair of Oriental vases, unmarked, 19th c.
Pair of Oriental vases with handles, unmarked, 19th c.
Ceramic pail, Oriental, 19th c.
Vase with floral decoration, German, early 20th c.
Carved bookends, Biltmore Industries, Asheville, American, c. 1905
Bronze elephant, probably French, 19th c.
Pair of bronze candlesticks, French, 19th c.
Pair of parrots, 19th c.
Multi-colored parrot, 19th c.
Footed ceramic jar, Chinese, 19th c.
Opaque glass vase, late 19th c.
Pair of covered vases, porcelain, unmarked, probably English, 19th c.
Pair of wood and brass candlesticks, 19th c.
Set of three matching stoneware vases, Japanese, 19th c.
Embracing couple, unglazed porcelain, unmarked, probably French, 19th c.
Pair of porcelain vases, made by Royal Worcester Co. for Tiffany and Co., English, late 19th c.
Pair of gentlemen, ivory, 19th c.
Two chargers, probably German, 19th c.
Vase, Chinese, 19th c.
Bronze bull, by Pierre-Jules Mene (1810-1871), French, 19th c.
Bronze horse and snake, by Jean-Francois-Theodore Gechter (1796-1844), French, 19th c.
Bronze bear attacked by hounds, by A.L. Bayre, French, 19th c.
Lacquerware swords, Japanese, bought by G.W. Vanderbilt on his trip to the Orient in 1892
Large brass container, Japanese, 19th c.
Table covers and pillows, 1989
Carpet, Oushak, Persian, 19th c.
Carpet, Sehna, Persian, 19th c.
Carpet, Kuba, Persian, 19th c.
Carpet, Ghendje, Persian, 19th c.
Carpet, Meshed, Persian, 19th c.
Carpet, Muhgul, Indian, 19th c.
Carpet, Caucasian, Southwest Caucasus (an area between the Black Sea and the Caspian Sea), 19th c.

SHERATON ROOM

FURNITURE:
Painted satinwood bed, English, 19th c.
Marquetry wardrobe, English, 19th c.
Double writing desk, English, 19th c.
Satinwood sidechair, English, 19th c.
Mahogany night stand, English, 19th c.
Satinwood washstand with marble top, English, 19th c.
Mahogany sidechairs & benches, English, 19th c.
Mahogany upholstered sofa, English, 19th c.
Two night stands, English, 19th c.

PAINTINGS & PRINTS:
Portraits left to right:
Gentleman, artist unknown, 19th c.
George, Frederick, and Eliza Vanderbilt, by Jacob H. Lazarus (1822-1891), American, c. 1870
Two Young Boys, artist unknown, c. 1860
Seascape, by M. Becketin, 19th c.
Miniature portrait of Harold S. Vanderbilt, youngest son of Alva and William K. Vanderbilt, inscription reads "Antoine Oderica d'apres Ch. Chaplin," 19th c.
Currier & Ives print of W.H. Vanderbilt and his trotters, American, 19th c.

DECORATIVE OBJECTS:
Poreclain Desk Set, Meissen, 19th c.
Mahogany arch timepiece English, 19th c.
Enamelled compote, Fie Boucheron, Palais Royal, French, 19th c.
Rock crystal & ormolu candlesticks, French, 19th c.
Brass inkwell, French, 19th c.
Two ivory letter openers, c. 1900
Lamp, late 19th c.
Photos of Edith Vanderbilt
Carpet, Persian, Khorassan tribe, 19th c.

SHERATON/CHIPPENDALE BATHROOM

Marble-topped dresser, 19th c.
Pair of painted chairs, Dutch, 19th c.
Table, 19th c.
Clothes hamper, 19th c.

CHIPPENDALE ROOM

FURNITURE:
Chippendale-style mahogany full tester bed, English, 19th c.
Neoclassical mahogany cabinet-on-chest, Dutch, 18th c.
Chippendale mahogany suite of seating furniture, English, 19th & 19th c.
Pair of mahogany candlestands, English, 19th c.
Mahogany bedside cupboard, English, 18th c.
Mahogany slant-front desk, English, 19th c.
Mahogany drop-leaf table, English, 19th c.
Painted leather magazine stand, 19th c.
Side table, English, 19th c.

PAINTINGS:
The Young Algerian Girl, by Pierre Auguste Renoir, French, 19th c.
Child with an Orange, by Pierre Auguste Renoir, French, c. 1881
Sortie du Port—Temps Lumineux, by Maxime Maufra (1861-1918), c. 1894, oil on canvas

View of Harbor in Sunset, by Maxime Maufra, 19th c., oil on canvas

Two watercolors, artist unknown, n.d.

DECORATIVE OBJECTS:
Mahogany bracket timepiece, Matthew Hill, English, early 19th c.
Pair of brass candlesticks, French, 18th c.
Three celedon vases, Chinese, Ch'ing Dynasty, Ch'ien-lung reign (1736-1796)
Pin cushion, Chinese, 19th c.
Two Oriental cloisonne covered containers, Chinese, 19th c.
Two sets of soapstone bookends
Ceramic cat on wooden stand, probably Chinese, 19th c.
Bed warmer, brass and copper, probably American, 19th c.
Brass dish, European
Brass fireplace set, 19th c.
Two lamps, 19th c.
Magazines, early 20th c.
Books, 19th c.
Carpet, Axminster or Wilton, English, 19th c.

CHIPPENDALE/OLD ENGLISH BATHROOM

Marble-topped sideboard, English, 19th c.
Two painted chairs, Dutch, 19th c.
Towel rack, 19th c.
Towels
Laundry hamper, 19th c.

OLD ENGLISH ROOM

FURNITURE:
Brass bed, English, 19th c.
Knole-style settee, 3 wing chairs, 4 side chairs, English, 19th c.
Oak gateleg table, English, 17th c.
Two Jacobean-style oak chests of drawers, English, 19th c.
Renaissance-style oak cupboard, 19th c.
Jacobean chest-on-stand, English, 17th c.
Stool, Biltmore Industries, Asheville, c. 1905
Gothic-style cupboard, 19th c.

PAINTINGS & PRINTS:
Left to right:
Lord Burghley, Cecil family ancestor, by Marc Gheeraerts, English, 1589
John Francis Amherst Cecil, by W.I. Cox (1900-1954)
William & Frances Cecil, by F. Zucchero (1543-1609), Spanish, 1599
Prints of English nobility, by Fiathorne, 17th c.

DECORATIVE OBJECTS:
Mantle timepiece, Andrew Flockart, London, c. 1820
Bronze stag, by P.J. Mene, French, 19th c.
Pair of celedon vases, China, Ch'ing Dynasty, Ch'ien-lung reign (1736-1796)
Three burlwood steins, Dutch, 18th c.
Petit point fireplace screen, American, 19th c.
Pair of brass candlebra, 19th c.
Walking cane, American or English, late 19th c.
Walking/hunting seat, American, 19th c.
Brass inlaid box, possibly Persian, 19th c.
Pewter teapot, French, 18th/19th c.
Pair of enameled candlesticks, Italian, 19th c.
Carpet, Persian, Hamadan district, 19th c.
Carpet, Persian, Sarab area, 19th c.

DOWNSTAIRS (Basement)

HALLOWEEN ROOM

Scale model of Biltmore House, Richard Morris Hunt, wood and paint, c. 1890

BOWLING ALLEY

Upholstered sofa and chairs, English, 19th c.
Two oak sofa tables, style of 17th c.
Octagon side table, 19th c.
Gateleg table, 19th c.
Dulcitone Player Piano, Cable Nelson Piano Co., Chicago
Piano bench, 19th c.
Handpainted dish, American, c. 1900
Ping pong table, 19th c.
Ping pong equipment, 19th c.
Photogravures, left to right: Dawn by Michelangelo, Night by Michelangelo, Venus de Milo, Sistine Ceiling by Michelangelo, Nike of Samothrace, St. George by Donatello, David by Michelangelo, and Lorenzo de' Medici by Michelangelo
Plaster casts, 19th c.
Table, 19th c.
Marble bust of George Washington Vanderbilt, by Mary Grant, English, c. 1900

SITTING AREA

Four dantesca chairs, Italian, 19th c.
Gateleg table, 19th c.
Trestle table, 19th c.
Settee, 19th c.

DRESSING ROOMS

Mahogany towel rack, 19th c.
Oak cabinet, 19th c.
Carved sidechairs, designed by R.M. Hunt and made by
    Baumgarten & Co. in New York, c. 1895
Assorted period clothes
Bowl and pitcher, porcelain, Minton & Spode, English,
    19th c.
Hair brush
Towels, 19th c.

MAIN DRESSING ROOM AND SHOWERS

Towel rack, Louis XV-style, 19th c.
Mahogany dressing table, English, 19th c.
Pierced back Sheraton-style chairs, 19th c.
Traveling toilet set, 19th c.
Gateleg table, 19th c.
Full-length mirror, 19th c.
Glassware, 19th c.
Bottle, 19th c.
Powder jar, 19th c.
Toilet set, porcelain, Minton & Spode, English, 19th c.

DRESSING ROOM LOUNGE

Carved settee with cane seat, style of 17th c., English,
    19th c.
Two carved side chairs, style of 17th c., English, 19th c.
Gateleg table, 19th c.
Assorted prints

GYMNASIUM

Spaulding parallel bars, 19th c.
Two Spaulding exercise machines, 19th c.
Spaulding Indian clubs, 19th c.
Wooden dumbbells, 19th c.
Wooden floor exercise machine, 19th c.
Fairbanks gym scale, 19th c.
Barbells, late 19th/early 20th c.
Cabinet, 19th c. with various exercise equipment and
    contents
Rowing machine, late 19th/early 20th c.

HOUSEKEEPER'S PANTRY

Walnut work table and stools, 19th c.
Period food can labels reproduced from the collection of
    Ralph and Terry Kovel, Cleveland, Ohio
Special thanks to American Can Co. for their contribution of
    custom cans for these labels

Stepping stool, 19th c.
Barrel, late 19th/early 20th c.
Oil lamp, 19th c.
Eye glasses, early 20th c.
Ink well, early 20th c.
Rug beater, early 20th c.

CANNING PANTRY

Period canning jars
Ball cold pack canner, 19th c.
Bottle capper, Farrow & Jackson Ltd., London, 19th c.
Cutlery chest, 19th c.
Oil lamps, 19th c. design
Kerosene tanks, The Davis Welding & Mfg. Co., Cincinnati,
    Ohio
Stepping stool, 19th c.
Tin box, 19th c.
"XXth Century" cooler, Cordley & Hayes, New York

SERVANTS' BEDROOMS

Six chestnut chests of drawers with mirror, American,
    19th c.
Six chestnut bedside tables, American, 19th c.
Iron washstands, American, 19th c.
Iron bedsteads, American, 19th c.
Splint seat rockers and sidechairs, American, 19th c.
Bathroom ware, Minton, England, late 19th c.
Several sets of servant's livery, 19th c.
Two chests of drawers, 19th c.
Wardrobe, 19th c.
Various prints
"The Gibson" mandolin, type "A", Gibson Guitar Co.,
    American, early 20th c.

PASTRY KITCHEN

Oak work table, 19th c.
Slat back splint seat chairs, 19th c.
Assorted copper molds, 19th c.
Wooden sifters
Cast iron cherry pitter, "Electric" brand
Universal bread maker, Landers, Frary & Clark, New Brit-
    ain, 1904
Brass & iron scale by American Cutlery Co., 19th c.
Bouche iron, 19th c.
Assorted period cooking utensils
Tin molds, early 20th c.
Garnet glass plates with gold trim, 19th c.
Ovens, Branhall, Deane & Co., New York
Refrigerator, Lorillard, New York

ROTISSERIE KITCHEN

Marble mortar and pestle, 19th c.
Oak work table, 19th c.
Sausage stuffer, early 20th c.
Cabinet, 19th c.
Iron tools
Copper pot
Rotisserie, Branhall, Deane Co., New York

MAIN KITCHEN

Copper pots and pans by Branhall & Deane Co., NY, 19th c.
Silvered server on wheels, A. Bertuch, Berlin W8
Enterprise coffee mill, Philadelphia, Pennsylvania, Patent
    Oct. 21, 1873
Enterprise sausage stuffer, Philadelphia, Pennsylvania
Marble mortar and pestle, 19th c.
Assorted period knives and choppers
Assorted period food tins
Copper pot, creamer, and sugar
Copper egg coddler
Oak work tables, 19th c.
Slat back splint seat chairs, 19th c.
Brass tray
Copper egg cups & tray
Scale
Ovens
Wooden bowls
Butcher block
Main table
Small table
Picnic basket
Leather travel/picnic cases
Grinder
Coal buckets

KITCHEN PANTRY AND DUMBWAITERS

Blue and white china by Mercer
Tray with copper water kettle, egg coddler, covered server,
    egg cups, and sauce pitcher
Breakfast set, Aynsley, England, 19th c.

SERVANTS' DINING ROOM

Rosewood and marble top sideboard, J. & J.W. Meeks, New
    York, 19th c.
Bentwood sidechairs, 19th c.
Oak sideboard, Mission style, 19th c.
Blue and white china by Mercer
Mahogany dining table, 19th c.
Oak and cane sidechair, American, 19th c.

Brass gong and beater, English, 1896. This gong was bought
    by Mr. Vanderbilt on Sept. 30, 1896 at the Army-Navy
    Co-Operative Society in London.
Oil lamps, 19th c.
Glassware, late 19th/early 20th c.
Flatware, Wallingford Co.
Prints, early 20th c. and modern reproductions

SERVANTS' HALL

Oak sideboard American, 19th c.
Splint seat and back rockers, made by L.J. Colony, Keene,
    New Hampshire, late 19th/early 20th c.
Carved oak drop front desk, Biltmore Industries, American,
    c. 1905
Slat-back, leather seat rockers, American, 19th c.
Mahogany trestle table, American, 19th c.
Corner bric-a-brac shelf, American, 19th c.
Three oak sidechairs, American, 19th c.
Oak work table, American, 19th c.
Mahogany octagon table, American, 19th c.
Ebony book shelf, American, 20th c.
Victrola, RCA, model VV-IX, hand crank, American, early
    20th c.
Zimmerman Autoharp, Dolgeville, New York
Folding oval table, American, 19th c.
Cane seat rocker, 19th c.
Hat rack, early 20th c.
Oil lamp, 19th c.
Checker board, c. 1900
Dogs, early 20th c.
Cats, early 20th c.
Prints, early 20th c. and modern reproductions
Letter box, late 19th c.
Vase, 19th c.
Covered dish, 19th c.

WALK-IN REFRIGERATORS

Turn of the century fruit crate labels
Milk cans
Special thanks to White Rock Bottling Co. for providing per-
    iod Sparkling Water bottles for display

SMALL PANTRY

Assorted period cans, boxes and barrels
Special thanks to Nabisco, Mortons Salt, Del Monte, Wm.
    Underwood Co., and Jerry and Audry Glenn for provid-
    ing items for display

TRUNK ROOM

Various late 19th c. and early 20th c. traveling trunks

FLORIST ROOM

Used for both flower arranging and storage of vases, baskets and flower-arranging essentials. Presently serves the same purpose

BROWN LAUNDRY

Washer, made by The Boss Washing Machine Co., Cincinnati, Ohio, early 20th c.
"Kingston" Anchor brand wringer, Lovell Manufacturing Co., Erie, Pennsylvania
"Old Time" wringer, The American Wringer Co., patent March 27, 1888
Two Crown fluting irons, patent Nov. 2, 1875
"Heat This" hand fluter, patent 1866
"The Best" hand fluter, H. Foote Man., Syracuse, New York
Assorted sad irons
Four "Mrs. Potts" detachable handle sad irons
Table size dampening press
Assorted sleeve boards and washboards
Oak work table, 19th c.
Slat back and rush seat chairs, 19th c.
Pot-bellied stove, late 19th c.

LAUNDRESSES' BATHROOM

Washstand, late 19th c.
Three cane seated rockers, 19th c.
Bowl & pitcher, 19th c.
Basket

MAIN LAUNDRY

Simplex Mangle, Algonquin, Illinois, patent May 30, 1911
The American Laundry Machinery Co., extractor, patent April 28, 1914
Troy Laundry Machinery Co., barrel washer, c. 1907
Troy laundry Machinery Co., drying racks, 1895
Oak work table, 19th c.
Slat-back chairs with splint seats, 19th c.
Assorted turn-of-the-century laundry aids

SMOKING ROOM

FURNITURE:
Two Knole-style sofas and three chairs, English, 19th c.
Carved mahogany Pembroke table, 19th c.
Walnut slant front desk, 19th c.
Carved side chair, 17th c.
Pembroke table with painted decorations, English, 19th c.

DECORATIVE OBJECTS:
Carved goat head pipe holder, 19th c.
Brass humidor, 19th c.
Pewter humidor, 19th c.
Small arch clock, English, 19th c.
Kovsh dish, Russian, 19th c.
Four majolica jugs, 19th c.
Delft inkstand, Dutch, 19th c.
Wedgwood portrait medallions, English, 18th c.
  Medallions on left: Queen Charlotte, Duke of York, Hamilton, Lavater, Shakespeare
  Medallions on right: Empress of Russia, Lord Nelson, Herschel, Pope, Captain Cook
Lacquer elephant with ivory figures, 19th c.
Lamp made from Japanese vase, 19th c.
Stuffed owl, 19th c.
Letter box, leather, with "GV" monogram, late 19th c.
Carpet, Persian, Bijar area, 19th c.

TROPHY ROOM

FURNITURE:
Marble top pedestal table, American, 19th c.
Four upholstered arm chairs, 19th c.
Sidechairs, 19th c.
End table, 17th c.
Side table, English, 18th c.

PRINTS:
Engravings by J. Reynolds and Ward

DECORATIVE OBJECTS:
Bronze fox, by Joseph-Victor Chemin (1825-1901), French, 19th c.
Bronze lioness, by Antoine-Louis Barye (1796-1875), French, 19th c.
Bronze buck and doe, by Pierre-Jules Mêne (1810-1871), French 19th c.
Bronze hunting dog, by P.J. Mêne, French, 19th c.
Silver trophy, won by Mrs. G.W. Vanderbilt for Best Harness Pair, American, 1903
Burlwood liquor box, American, 19th c.
Basket, early 20th c.
Photos of Vanderbilt family members and friend
Box of poker chips and cards, 19th c.
Box with ivory chips, Tiffany & Co., American, 19th c.
Pair of marble lamps, early 20th c.
Fireplace set, 19th c.
Assorted mounted birds and animals
Carpet, Caucasian, Karabagh area, 19th c.
Carpet, Persian, Qashgai area, 19th c.

BACHELORS' HALLWAY

FURNITURE:
Two leather armchairs, Jacobean-style, English, 19th c.
Two gateleg tables, American, 19th c.
Oak desk, Louis XV provincial-style, 19th c.
Oak cabinet, Louis XV provincial-style, 19th c.
Walnut credenza and matching stands, Renaissance-revival style, 19th c.
Mahogany and brass coffer chest, 19th c.
Two *dantesca*-style chairs, Biltmore Furniture Conservation Shop, 1987
Portuguese/Spanish arm chair

DECORATIVE OBJECTS:
Victrola, RCA, credenza model, American, patented 1904
Striking clock, by Robert Harlow, Ashbourne, England
Architectural prints, European scene, by Axel Haig (1838-1921), Swedish, 19th c.
Young mounted bear, American, 19th c.

THE STABLE

REPAIR ROOM

Two harness cleaning and repair racks, American, 19th c.
Leather working tools, American, 19th c.
Table, American, c. 1900
Splint rocking chair, American, 19th c.
Horse collar, c. 1900
Pony collar, early 20th c.
Tool box, late 19th c.
Saddle repair horse, reproduction in 19th c. style, Biltmore Furniture Conservation Shop, 1987
Chest of drawers, American, 19th c.
Small round table, American, 19th c.
Harnesses, late 19th/early 20th c.
Lanterns, late 19th/early 20th c.
Bridles, late 19th/early 20th c.
Girth, late 19th/early 20th c.

BLANKET ROOM

Four blue quarter blankets with G.W. Vanderbilt monogram, 19th c.
Four carriage lap blankets, one monogrammed, 19th c.
Cedar-lined blanket trunk, 19th c.
Blanket trunk, reproduction of 19th c. style, Biltmore Furniture Conservation Shop, 1987
Two sets of fitted horse clothing, American, c. 1900
Roller, American, early 20th c.
Table, American, c. 1900
Solid leather box muzzle, American, late 19th c.

SADDLE ROOM

Gentleman's saddle, c. 1900
Pony saddle, late 19th c.
Three sidesaddles, 19th c.
Pack saddle, c. 1900
Two girth stretchers, reproductions of 19th century style, Biltmore Furniture Conservation Shop, 1987
Saddle airer, reproduction of 19th c. style, Biltmore Furniture Conservation Shop, 1987
Table, c. 1900
Bridles, modern (late 20th c.)
Girths, modern (late 20th c.)
Stirrups, stirrup leathers, modern (late 20th c.)
Stable steps, 19th c.
Saddle repair horse, reproduction of 19th c. style, Biltmore Furniture Conservation Shop, 1987
Riding crop, 19th c.

HARNESS ROOM

Set of harness, late 19th c.
Harness cleaning and repair rack, American, 19th c.
Brass sponge rack, c. 1895
Cast iron stove "Ranger Windsor No. 27", c. 1900
Set of hames, 20th c.
Hanging wall cabinet, reproduction of 19th c. style, Biltmore Furniture Conservation Shop, 1987
Bits and stirrups, modern (late 20th c.)
Equestrian top hat with leather traveling case, early 20th c.
Riding boots, leather, with accompanying stretchers, English, early 20th c.
Hunting crop with bone handle, sterling silver mounts, English, c. 1890
Buggy whip, wood, c. 1900
Buggy whip, wood, sterling silver handle, inscribed with monogram of Cornelia S. Vanderbilt, 1916
Lap blanket, wool, late 19th/early 20th c.
Harness vise, meant to be wall-mounted, American, patented 1902
Carriage jack, American, c. 1890
Carriage socket set, American, c. 1890
Singeing lamp, brass, an alcohol or oil burning lamp used to remove horse hair during cleaning, 1890
Carriage lantern, c. 1890
Buggy wheel repair tools, American, patented 1883

We bespeak the visitors' patience, should any object not be found in the exact spot described. As in all homes, housekeeping does involve rearrangements.

BIBLIOGRAPHY

Biltmore Estate, the Vanderbilt Family, and Related Subjects:

Auchincloss, Louis. *The Vanderbilt Era: Profiles of a Gilded Age.* New York: Charles Scribner's Sons, 1989.

Baker, Paul. *Richard Morris Hunt.* Cambridge, MA: MIT Press, 1980.

Girouard, Mark. *The Victorian Country House.* New Haven: Yale University Press, 1979.

Hoyt, Edwin P. *The Vanderbilts and their Fortunes.* New York: Doubleday and Co., 1962.

Pandich, Susanne and Dennis R. Dodds. "George W. Vanderbilt's Collection of Oriental Rugs at Biltmore Estate." *HALI, The International Journal of Oriental Carpets and Textiles,* Vol. 3, no. 4, 1981.

Roper, Laura Wood. *FLO: A Biography of Frederick Law Olmsted.* Biltmore: John Hopkins Univ. Press, 1973.

Schenck, Carl A. *The Birth of Forestry in America: Biltmore Forest School, 1898-1913.* Forest History Society and Appalachian Consortium, Santa Cruz, CA: 1974.

Sloan, Florence A. *Maverick in Mauve.* New York: Doubleday and Co., 1983.

Stein, Susan R., ed. *The Architecture of Richard Morris Hunt.* Univ. of Chicago Press, 1986.

Stevenson, Elizabeth. *Park Maker: A Life of Frederick Olmsted.* New York: MacMillan & Co., 1977.

Ward, Susan and Ewer, Patricia. "Tapestry Conservation at Biltmore House." *The International Journal of Museum Management and Curatorship,* Butterworths and Co., Ltd., Volume 7, no. 8, December 1988.

Stable:

Hugget, Frank E. *Carriages at Eight: Horse-drawn Society in Victorian and Edwardian Times.* Fakenham, Norfolk, England: Fakenham Press Ltd., 1979.

Moseman's Illustrated Guide for the Purchasers of Horse Furnishing Goods. New York: C.M. Moseman and Brother, 1892.

Underhill, Francis T. *Driving for Pleasure; Or, the Harness Stable and Its Appointments.* New York: D. Appleton and Co., 1897. Reproduced by Unigraphic, Inc., Evansville, Ind., 1980.

CORNELIA AND EDITH VANDERBILT, c. 1906